CW00819489

PUNK ON 45

REVOLUTIONS ON VINYL
1976-79

PUNK ON 45

REVOLUTIONS ON VINYL
1976-79

Gavin Walsh

Text by Paul A. Woods

Plexus, London

Dedicated to the late, great Joe Strummer

All rights reserved including the right of
reproduction in whole or in part in any form
Copyright © 2006 by Plexus Publishing Limited
Published by Plexus Publishing Limited
25 Mallinson Road
London SW11 1BW
www.plexusbooks.com

British Library Cataloguing In Publication Data

Walsh, Gavin
    Punk on '45 : revolutions on vinyl 1976-79
    1.Punk rock music 2. Art and music 3.Sound recordings -
    - Album covers
    I.Title
    741.6'6

ISBN-10: 0-85965-370-6
ISBN-13: 978-0-85965-370-1

Printed and bound by Bookprint, Spain
Book and cover design by Rebecca Longworth

This book is sold subject to the condition that it shall
not by way of trade or otherwise be lent, re-sold, hired out
or otherwise circulated without the publisher's prior consent
in any form of binding or cover other than that in which it is
published and without a similar condition including this
condition being imposed on the subsequent purchaser.

CONTENTS

the stooges

elektra
INT. 80209

1969
REAL COOL TIME

INTRODUCTION

'Ripped and torn.' 'Cut and paste.' 'Blank generation.' 'Do it yourself.' It's easier to come up with clichés to describe punk rock's visual aesthetic than to define what punk itself actually *was*.

Which is why the pictures in *Punk on 45* are going to do most of the talking. But first, a little history: 1976 was no Year Zero, no matter what the more Stalinist spikyheads claimed at the time. Both the musical and visual back-to-brass-tacks approach had antecedents in the 1960s beat boom. Think of all those Beatles/Stones/Animals EP's with picture sleeves from your parents' record collection. (Or your grandparents', if you truly are a snotty young thing.) Now think of that famous shot of Johnny Rotten flipping the finger to a pic sleeve of the Fab Four, and put your own finger on what changed betwixt the two eras: *attitude*.

The US bands now regarded as protopunks, like the Stooges and the MC5, were visually presented like any other young rock'n'rollers: group line-up, left to right, watch the birdie. Now scowl for the camera. For the

They may have long hair, but they're nothing but no-good punks: The Stooges in 1969, the year of their epochal first recordings, featuring a young 'Iggy Stooge' (bottom right of sleeve) (1).

only element that separates Elektra's cover for the first Stooges LP from that of their elder labelmates the Doors is that Iggy and the gang seem palpably pissed off. The single from the album that co-opts the same cover image, '1969', is the ultimate 1960s statement in every sense – it came not to praise the era of Beatlemania and Vietnam, but to bury it. 'War across the USA,' snarled a young Iggy Pop (nee Stooge) of his nation's civil unrest – and still these nihilistic brats complained that they were bored.

It comes over in the classic cover shot – a 'yeah, whatever' surliness that became the template for American garage bands up to the Dictators, the Ramones, the Dead Boys and beyond. These boys looked like no-goodniks, they had unkempt hair and biker jackets, but they weren't hippies. They were what Middle America (and, in admiring terms, Iggy himself) would regard as a neighbourhood threat; nothing but cheap *punks*.

In the UK, where the imported term 'punk' would acquire more specific subcultural connotations, the pub-rock scene was the back-to-basics movement of the mid-1970s. Its basis was traditional guitar-led R&B, just like the beat-boom/British invasion bands of the mid-1960s. The main difference is that these weren't bright young things forging a way forward in 'Swinging London', but hard-nosed young men reacting against the prissiness and pretensions of the 1970s rock scene. As prosaic as a beer bottle in the teeth, some of the pub rockers took the historic step of stressing their parochial origins: bands like Kilburn and the High Roads and the Hammersmith Gorillas had names that seemed to fall off of London street signs. Their (mostly monochrome) picture sleeves unconsciously reflected the greyness of 1970s Britain, where the only relief for these unsmiling young men lay in booze, diet pills

and rock'n'roll.

Meanwhile, in New York City, the new minimalism attached itself to groups of young musicians who, for the first time, came under the collective banner of 'punk rock'. But this was a broad church, not yet defined by the criteria of speed, minimalism and snotty arrogance that later held sway. It was also remarkable in that it marked the point where women truly stepped up to the podium – not as backing singers, decoration, or as women playing a man's game, but as performers every part as perverse, compelling or abrasive as their male cohorts.

Coined by rock journalist Lenny Kaye, the term 'punk rock' would follow him into the Patti Smith Group, but it first denoted the young, loud and semi-competent mid-Sixties garage bands collected on his definitive compilation album, *Nuggets*. By the time it was adapted to describe the underground bar-band scene at CBGB's and Max's Kansas City, 'punk rock' as a label was so widely applied as to be almost meaningless.

The vast gulf between the performers can be seen on some of their pic sleeves: Poets and experimentalists like Patti Smith and Tom Verlaine of Television took their cues from mid-60s Dylan, the Velvet Underground and the poet Rimbaud, every inch the pale and interesting artists. The Ramones took the slouching, leather-jacketed street-punk appeal of the Stooges and made it cartoonishly uniform. Deborah Harry of Blondie was a pouting, coquettish Ronnie Spector doused in peroxide, while Wayne County was a gender-bending hangover from the glitter era, like a New York Doll on oestrogen shots.

Perhaps the main unifying factor came in the shape of Richard Hell – formerly of Television and the Heartbreakers, by 1977 leader of his own band of gutter-poets the Voidoids. Progenitor of the 'ripped and torn' look, Hell was the first to apply a raggedly aus-

1

2

The third and fourth singles by The MC5 (1 & 2), 1970. Though the band were longhairs and singer Rob Tyner was an afro'd hippie, their radical politics, speed and aggression predated bands like The Clash.

tere (and impoverished) chic to his tufted hair and his clothes. Although never a mass media legend, the New York punk left his mark when, according to him, unorthodox London clothing retailer Malcolm McLaren made mental notes and took the look transatlantic. Spiky, gelled hair and ripped Oxfam (or Goodwill, in the US) clothes became *de rigeur* among London's original punks – at first a shocking stylistic innovation, later something of a uniform.

As for the 'punk rockers' (this being a term imported by the UK music press via Lenny Kaye and decried by, of all significant figures, John Rotten/Lydon), when their wares first spewed out onto the market their visual appeal was based solely on the threatening arrogance of youth. The Damned's 'New Rose', a moronically enjoyable Stooges pastiche, was the first UK single to be officially deemed 'punk', as opposed to, say, pub rockers Eddie and the Hot Rods' 'Teenage Depression'. Its visual appeal lay in a b/w photo of the Damned themselves – less moody but leerier than the pub bands, it seemed to bear out their reputation as a disreputable bunch of herberts (in the nicest British tradition, of course).

From the end of 1976, with the release of the Sex Pistols' epochal 'Anarchy In The UK', the floodgates were open. The printing presses spewed out pic sleeves as big corporate labels and overnight independents alike pressed seven-inches by the truckload. All the original bands in the classic British wave of punk were defined, at least in part, by their visual appeal. The Clash initially came across as stern young agitprop guerillas in slogan-painted clothes, set against a menacing urban backdrop of a depressed London. If all imagery is propaganda, then The Clash sold the idea that urban Britain wasn't facing an economic recession so much as an apocalypse.

But the main players sold themselves in an entirely

different manner. It's ironic, perhaps, that the Pistols, via tabloid shock stories, became instantly recognisable icons of a movement their vocalist later denied all kinship with. Look at their original pic sleeves, however, and see how the Situationist attitudinising of McLaren and playful creativity of Jamie Reid was less concerned with pop icons than iconoclasm. There's nary a band line-up shot to be seen, at least on the original pressings. Instead, the Pistols established the punk (and early post-punk) tradition that all images of respectability and mundanity could be subverted; that cheerful normality was essentially sinister, concealing the festering sickness beneath insipidly smiling British (and Western) culture.

The Buzzcocks, though first seen pressed together in all their monochrome glory for the DIY classic *Spiral Scratch* EP, cleaved to a similarly faceless identity – at least as far as single covers went. Like their music, they were subtler than the raging electric snarl of the Pistols. Designed by Malcolm Garrett in a style that combined advertising and pop art, its earliest manifes-

The 1978 classic 'Cheree' (3) by Suicide. Formed in 1972, the radical sound of Alan Vega on vocals and Martin Rev on keyboard was too 'punk' for the audience on a Clash support slot – who showed their appreciation with cans and bottles.

tation, 'Orgasm Addict', featured artwork by Linder Sterling (later of Manchester art-punk band Ludus) inspired by Dada and exemplifying punk's cut-and-paste/Do It Yourself ethos. The appeal of such gaudy/austere graphics would permeate the 1980s, that style-obsessed decade when maverick visual piracy would be incorporated, like mostly everything else, into the corporate mainstream.

But back in the late 1970s, these were the visual emblems of the punk generation. And as the DIY philosophy mushroomed, countless independent labels like Step Forward, Deptford Fun City and, later, the more enduring Rough Trade and Beggars Banquet came into their own. By 1977, punk singles had become a major British cottage industry (with the US by now a few steps behind). According to your perspective, it was either the greatest grassroots musical eruption since skiffle, or, according to Mark E. Smith of The Fall (who came out of that same era), it was 'the '77 shit pile'. In truth, it was a little bit of both.

But it wasn't only the indies (to use the latter-day vernacular) who flooded the market. Relatively major labels (for a short period at least) all indulged their pet punk bands, to the point of giving their releases a very specific visual identity: Chrysalis marketed Generation X as the dayglo revivalists they were, with Warholish saturated colours giving a look more vibrant than the reheated powerpop they played; more interesting were X Ray Spex, signed to mainstream UK giant EMI (who, having first signed and dropped the Pistols, were desperate not to miss out again) – based around young singer Poly Styrene's semi-psychedelic lyrics about the consumer society, theirs was an altogether different shade of dayglo.

These 'big names' aside, monochrome and grey were often the primary colours of the independent punk scene. Numerous singles here by long forgotten (or unknown) bands exhibit the self-conscious side of the DIY ethic. Never have amateurism and bargain basement production values been flouted so unapologetically. This was Xerox machine culture, long before the days when kids could harness scanners to their home PC. If

an image looked as if it was stolen from elsewhere, downgraded and murky, then it was, by extension, so much more 'authentic'. By virtue of repetition, certain punk visual aesthetics became a cliché. If graphic designs or sleeve illustrations were drab, or depressing, or stolen from an instruction manual, that was arguably the point. And never before had the British high street provided so many cheap Kodak images. Amusement arcades, decrepit dancehalls and bingo halls, all were backdrops for the band to shuffle by or slouch against, supposedly a testament to their *street* credibility.

There were still some subversively creative sensibilities at work, and these can be seen in the cut-and-paste sleeve designs juxtaposing the bizarre and the disturbing with the mundane. Skeletons with psychedelic eyes gaze upon tower blocks; 'found images' of gas masks and militarism suggest the apocalyptic dread that would flower in the immediate post-punk era. The unashamed artiness of many of the post-punk bands – Magazine, Joy Division – also brought a surreal, almost Gothic (*sans* big hair/eyeliner connotations) design style to their 45 rpm existential nightmares.

On a smaller scale, this vein of DIY surrealism crept back across the USA. (Where it had actually originated, in early single cover designs by Pere Ubu and the obscure but hip Electric Eels.) While most US 'punkers' were represented by standard shots of the band leaning against walls, with low-slung guitars, etc, there is a colder *frisson* to covers like those of the Weirdos' 'We Got The Neutron Bomb' or the Dadaistics' 'Paranoia Perception'. Their juxtaposition of found images and satirical intent comes, after all, from the mighty nation where clean-cut suburban conformity lives happily alongside the greatest military death machine the world has ever known.

Further examples of this sinister art-school ethic can be found in the dying days of 1970s punk, with post-punk bands like The Cure (later a huge cult) and Punishment of Luxury (now forgotten and hugely underrated). But that's as far as it went. Always difficult to define, by the end of the 1970s punk rock had devolved into its *reductio ab absurdum*. Defined once again by its bottom line of youth, speed and arrogance, 'authentic' punk was represented by the football terrace aggression of the 'Oi!' movement in the UK, and the grinding steamroller of hardcore in the US. More so than ever, 'punk' was visually represented by pictures of snarling young men with very short hair.

Oi! and hardcore did what they were intended to do, and no more. Any renaissance of visual subversion or cut-and-paste creativity seemed mostly beside the point – which was, for working-class angry brigades ranging from the East End's Cockney Rejects to the West Coast's Black Flag, that they were 'for real'. And so ended an era. Except, perhaps, for stirrings to the east of London and in the UK's more obscure rural environs. For punk was not just a youth cult to the anarchist faithful of the Crass collective, but an alternative lifestyle to be strictly and ideologically adhered to. But that is another era and another story . . .

And today? It's a stock response for people who lived through the punk years to say 'it's like punk never happened'. While it never delivered (and rarely promised) the Revolution, however, in pop-cultural terms it casts a shadow everywhere. Bands like the US's Green Day and the Distillers have resurrected the speed and aggression of punk, while the UK's Arctic Monkeys

New York's most androgynous: promo single 'Trash' and 'Jet Boy', from the NY Dolls' eponymous 1973 debut (1 & 2), and the Japanese release of 'Stranded In The Jungle' from 1974's Too Much Too Soon (3). Their antithesis, poet Patti Smith, was still a rock'n'roll traditionalist – as shown by her 1974 and 76 covers of Hendrix's 'Hey Joe' (4), Them's 'Gloria' and The Who's 'My Generation' (5).

DR.FEELGOOD
She's A Windup

2

and Franz Ferdinand have matched it to the jagged angularity of the artier post-punk bands that followed.

But punk aesthetics are equally detectable in other aspects of pop culture: in low-budget guerrilla filmmaking, late-night TV, advertising, and even, on occasion, in CD cover design. Now that Johnny Rotten is no longer a threat to the moral fibre of Western youth, but a reality TV star, the punk era can be seen for what it was: a volatile upsurge of youthful creativity, some of it iconoclastic and groundbreaking, some of it embarrassingly naïve and inept. Memories are made of this. And this book is a collective visual memory of the punk era.

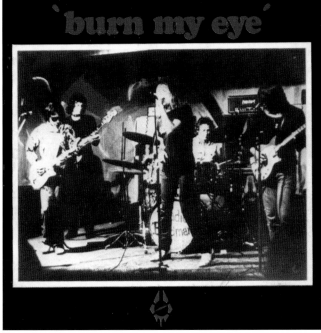

3

By the time of this Kilburn and the High Roads retrospective (1), singer Ian Dury (bottom left of sleeve) was playing to the same young audiences as the punks who'd copped some of his attitude. Pre-punk but not prehistory: Brit pub rockers Dr Feelgood weathered the 1977 punk storm with hard-edged R&B like 'She's A Windup' (2); Burn My Eye, 1976 debut EP by Radio Birdman, the Australian wanna-be Stooges (3).

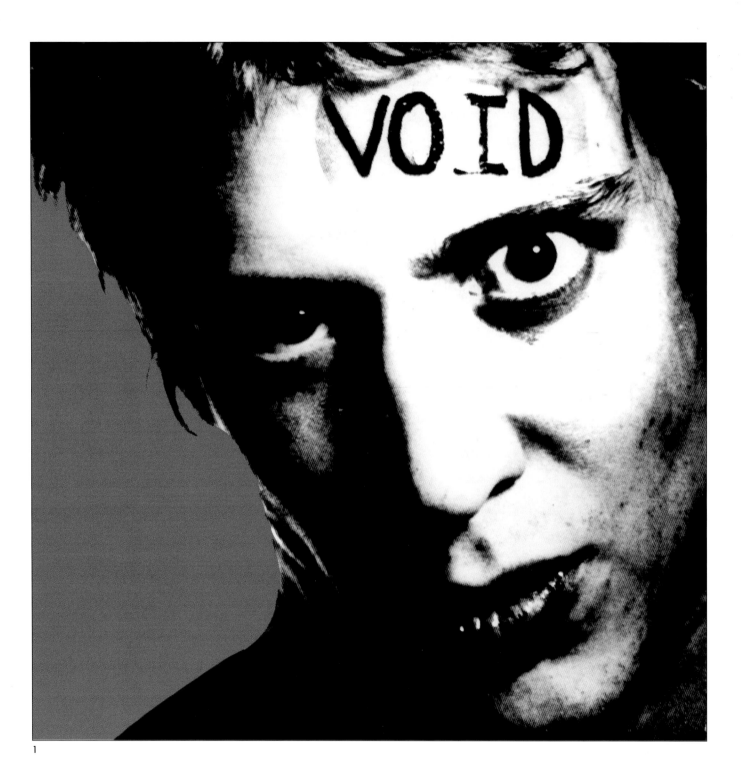

1

CHAPTER 1

ORIGINAL US PUNK

It's a small irony that the term 'punk rock' originated in the USA. It's only now, well over three decades since the term was first applied, that there's any consensus as to what it actually means. It was first coined by Lenny Kaye (later Patti Smith's guitarist) to describe three-chord wonders like Question Mark and the Mysterians and the Standells who sprang up, in the mid-Sixties, in response to the Beatles/Stones-led 'British invasion'. Most of these bands had their greatest (or only) hits anthologised on Kaye's original 1972 *Nuggets* collection, which spawned a whole sub-genre of compilation albums.

Several years on, in the mid-1970s, the definition of 'punk' changed somewhat. It was largely a cultural and geographical accident that editor/publisher John Holmstrom chose to call his New York-based magazine *Punk*, centring on Lower Manhattanite performers and newcomers in the clubs CBGB's and Max's Kansas City. All that was essential was that they shared he

Richard Hell filled a void in popular culture, his ripped 'n' torn style crossing the Atlantic to influence UK punk. This is the Live At CBGB's *EP (1), named after the New York club where the US punk scene began.*

and his buddies' love of trash culture and contempt for the self-righteous hippie generation. By default, both NY's elder statesman of decadence, Lou Reed, and performers left over from the glitter era like Wayne County (and the Electric Chairs) and the Heartbreakers (featuring Johnny Thunders and Jerry Nolan, ex-New York Dolls) would fall under the all-encompassing 'punk' umbrella. By 1974, the only band playing the underground bar and club scene that existed totally independently of what came before was the Dictators – funny, loud and brash, they celebrated US trash culture. As Legs McNeil of *Punk* said to Jon Savage about the Dictators, 'We all had the same reference points: White Castle hamburgers, muzak, malls.'

But that was far from the whole story. In Cleveland, Ohio, born in an absolute cultural void, Pere Ubu (named after the infamous play *Ubu Roi* by symbolist author Alfred Jarry) produced a sound that combined musical minimalism and surreal lyrics. First released on their homegrown independent Hearthan/Hearpen label, it had little affinity to anything else in rock music, but the post-punk world would at least offer them a place to

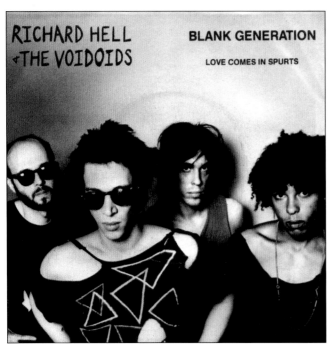

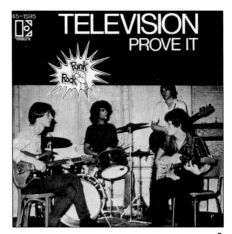

The lineage of US punk: Before Richard Hell coined the term 'Blank Generation', he co-founded Television with Tom Verlaine, seen at the foreground on 1977's 'Marquee Moon' (1). After a brief spell with the Heartbreakers, he struck out with the Voidoids to release 'Blank Generation' (2). The 'punk rock' label used by Elektra to sell the Spanish 'Prove It' (3) is deceptive, given the rather cerebral music. The ultra rare Japanese issue of 'Venus' presents the band in typical punk style backs against the wall in black and white (4). Much faster and rawer was the 1978 cover of Iggy and the Stooges' 'Search And Destroy' by the Dictators (5), trash-culture soul-mates of the Ramones – who, by the time of 1978's 'Don't Come Close' (6), seemed to have made the transition into cartoon characters courtesy of Punk magazine's John Holstrom.

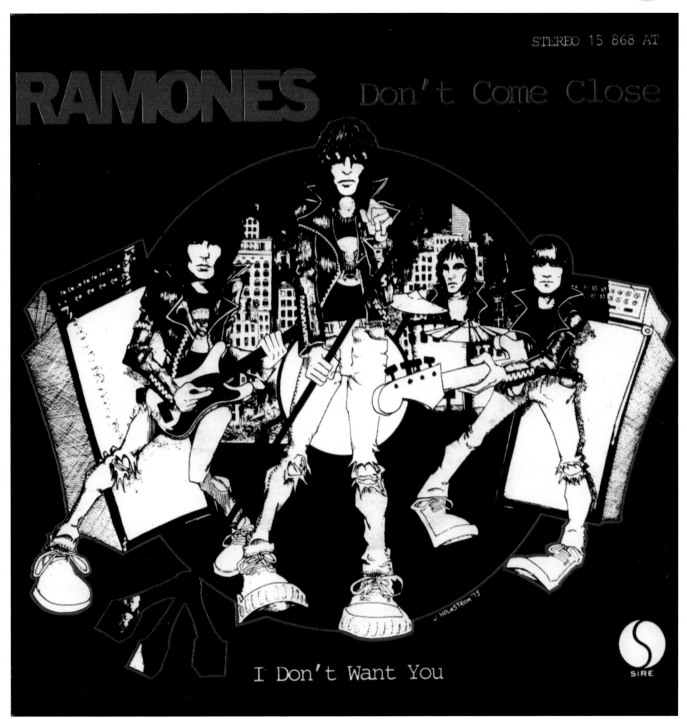

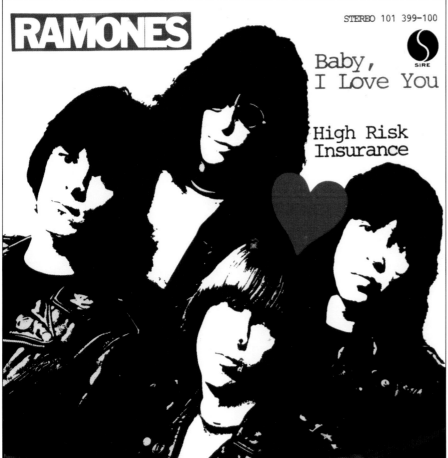

RAMONES

STEREO 101 399-100

Baby,
I Love You

High Risk
Insurance

2

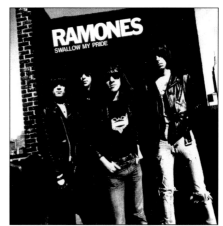

3

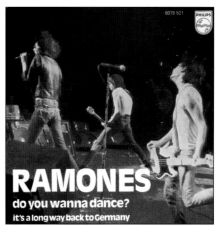

4

The Ramones set the template for speed, brevity and trashiness. From 1977's 'Sheena Is A Punk Rocker' (1) and 'Swallow My Pride' (3) to covers of Johnny Rivers' 'Do You Wanna Dance?' (4, Dutch edition and 5, Japanese) and their 1980 version of the Ronettes' 'Baby I Love You' (2), they remained the same be-sneakered corporate entity – even after swapping drummer Tommy Ramone for Marky Ramone.

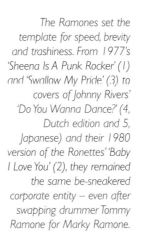

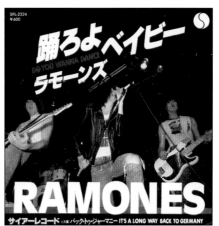

5

blondie

denis
contact in red square
kung fu girls

1

blondie

denis
contact in red square
kung fu girls

2

Blondie's popularity swiftly grew, from their 1976 small label debut 'X Offender' (2), to global editions of chart-topping singles such as the Japanese and French issues of 'Denis' (3 & 4) and the Japanese release of 'Heart of Glass' (5), which put the peroxide siren on the bedroom walls of teenage boys everywhere.

(1) and (2): Deborah Harry is presented in pencil-browed ice maiden guise on the alternate blue/red covers of 'Denis' (1977).

2

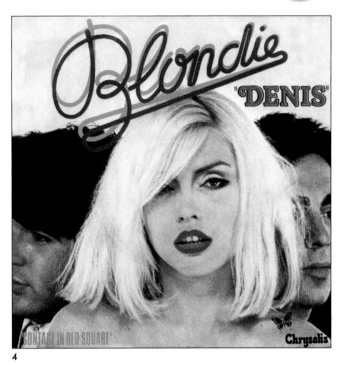

4

3

5

1

2

3

4

On the 1977 Dutch edition of
'Denis' (1) and the UK release
of 'Picture This' (5) Blondie
were only 'punk' in as far as
the word related to 1960s
pop and garage music. By the
time of their 1978 disco-
influenced hit 'Heart of Glass'
(4) and 1979's 'Sunday Girl'
(2, and French language
version, 3) they had staked
out a pop music niche of their
own, predating Madonna,
Gwen Stefani and lesser
impersonators.

plough their unique furrow. No such succour for their Cleveland compatriots the Electric Eels: fuelled by hate and nihilism, reputedly dressed in ripped clothes held together by safety pins, they were 'punk' before their time, in a cultural milieu that couldn't sustain them. They imploded in mid-1975, many of their distortion-wracked recordings not seeing the light of day until years later.

But in New York City, at least people were listening. The lineage that began in 1973 with the Neon Boys – well-educated kids playing dumb 1960s punk music, led by two expatriates from Kentucky – took some twists and turns that came to epitomise the breadth of the so-called movement. The Neon Boys mutated into Television, led by young Southern literati Tom Verlaine (nee Miller) and Richard Hell (nee Meyers), who cut the quasi-psychedelic garage rock single 'Little Johnny Jewel' in 1975 on Ork, which, as with Pere Ubu's label, was one of the tiny independents (named after its proprietor, Terry Ork) which predated the punk era. Hell had already written a song which became emblematic of the punk scene, 'Blank Generation', but was ousted from the band due to his lack of technical ability on bass.

Hitching up with the Heartbreakers, who played more basic three-chord rock'n'roll, for several months, Hell's songs were finally given a proper airing with his own band, the Voidoids. Always more of a critical than a commercial suc-

1

2

The German edition of the first Talking Heads single, 'Love Goes To Building On Fire' from 1977 (1), boasts the legend 'Original New York Punk Rock'. With the original line-up of David Byrne, Tina Weymouth and Chris Frantz, the cerebral funksters showed that 'punk' could be a rarefied thing. 'Psycho Killer' (2) and 'Pulled Up' (3) were tracks from their Talking Heads '77 debut album, released as singles with arty original archive photos on the sleeves.

3

This French edition of 'Psycho Killer' (4), the song most identified with Talking Heads during the 1970s, features a singularly personal interpretation of the song by an unidentified French artist. While the lyric is an agitated portrayal of a psychotic becoming violent, this surreal image cryptically evokes both war and the male sex organ. 'Qu'est que c'est?' indeed.

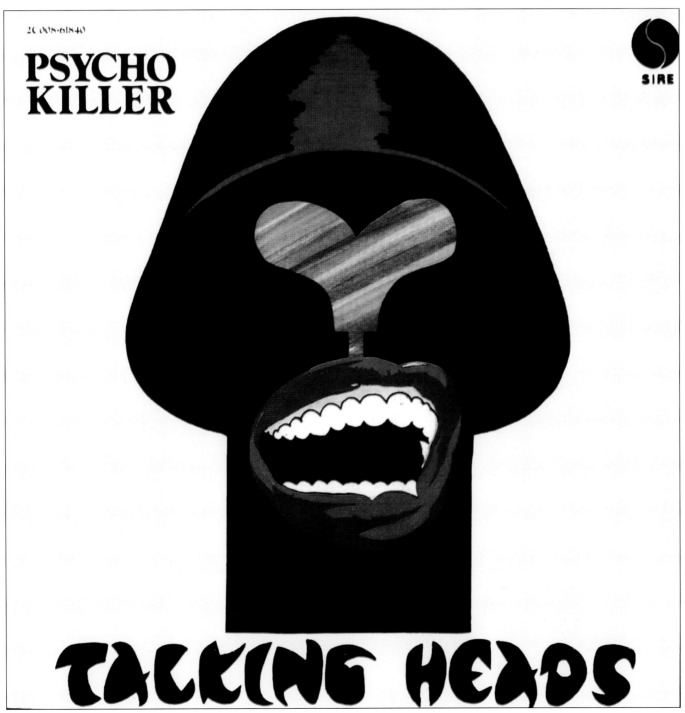

1

3

4

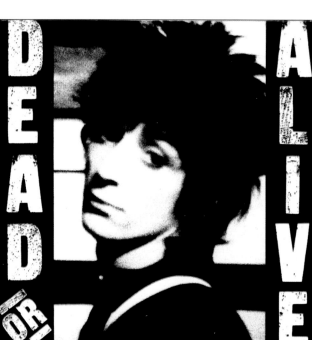

2

Wayne County & The Backstreet Boys

5

Live from Max's Kansas City: ex-NY Dolls Johnny Thunders and Jerry Nolan formed the Heartbreakers, whose 1977 singles 'One Track Mind' and 'Born To Lose' (1 & 3) were recorded amidst the UK punk scene; ex-Doll Arthur 'Killer' Kane released 'Mr Cool' the same year (4), while Thunders went solo with 1978's 'Dead Or Alive' (2). Former Max's compatriot Wayne County paid tribute to the venue in 1976 (5); in 1977 he came to the UK with toilet-rock band the Electric Chairs to record 'Fuck Off' (6), 1978's ted-punk love song 'Eddie and Sheena' (7) and the Blatantly Offensive EP (8). By now, Wayne wasn't trying too hard in the drag queen stakes – though it was only a short time before he donned frocks and re-emerged as Jayne County.

6

7

8

cess, he had already made his transatlantic mark by this time – when maverick rag trader Malcolm McLaren incorporated Hell's improvised 'ripped-and-torn' look into the designs created by him and Vivienne Westwood for their boutique Sex, on London's Kings Road. (In their 1986 'Tenth Anniversary of Punk' issue, *NME* would run Hell's account of the misappropriation under the heading, 'I Wuz Robbed!')

Meanwhile, Verlaine's onetime girlfriend Patti Smith had made the full transition from occasionally performing poetess and fringe theatre actress to rock'n'roll poet. In her 29th year, her extraordinary album *Horses* (1975)

was released to a mix of critical acclaim and bemusement. She was, according to those rock journalists who'd cottoned on to the new term, 'the Priestess of Punk'.

How amorphous this term was became apparent when it was also applied (perhaps more aptly) to the Ramones: four pretend 'brudders' from Queens, NY, who took the cacophonic thrash of the Dolls and the trash-culture infatuation of the Dictators and reduced them down to tunefully brutal two-minute pop songs. It set the punk template for speed and disaffected surliness. By the time the Ramones crossed the Atlantic to play London for the first time, in 1976, they would find an

PUNK
ON 45

2

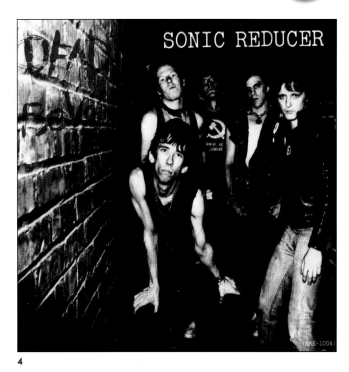

4

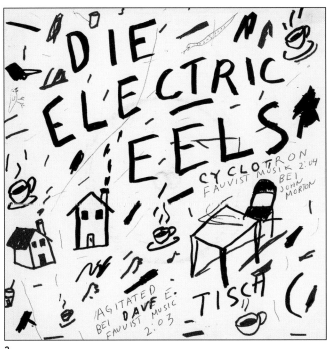

3

5

29

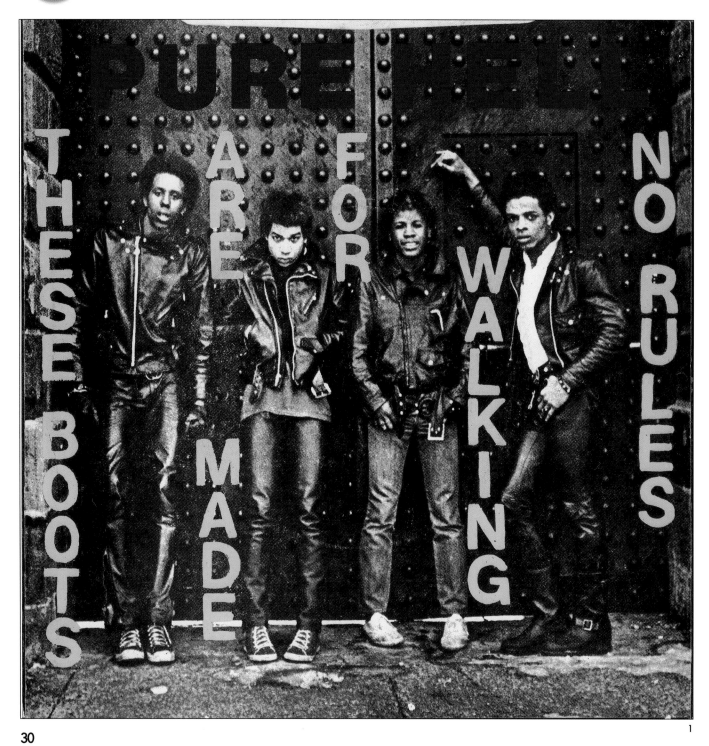

Pages 28-29: Cleveland (punk) rocks: Cleveland art rockers Pere Ubu recorded '30 Seconds Over Tokyo' in 1975 (1) and 1978's 'The Modern Dance' (2) for their own Hearthan/Hearpen label. The Electric Eels' 'Cyclotron'/'Agitated' (3) was also recorded in 1975 but, frighteningly ahead of its time, not released by Rough Trade until 1979. Members of both bands also played in Rocket From the Tombs – as did members of the Dead Boys, whose 1977 singles 'Sonic Reducer' (4) and rare Japanese version 'Tell Me' (5) are the nearest the US had come to the snotty attitude of the Pistols at that time.

Pure Hell – who covered 'These Boots Are Made For Walking' in 1978 (1) – were the first black punk band. Later member Neon Leon earned a footnote in history when he dropped in on Sid and Nancy at the Chelsea Hotel, the night Ms Spungen died. Right: Punk teen queens or Suzi Quatro revisited? The Runaways were put together by maverick Svengali Kim Fowley, releasing 'Cherry Bomb' (2) and the Blackmail EP (3) in 1977 and 'School Days' (4) the following year.

2

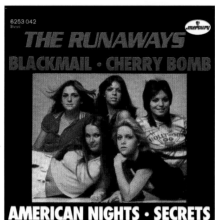

3

4

appreciative audience, many of whom were forming their own bands. They were by then, as Joe Strummer of The Clash later acclaimed, 'the daddy of all punk bands'.

And still the New York definition of punk was wide enough to encompass Deborah Harry and her boyfriend Chris Stein's band, Blondie. While they shared the Ramones' 1960s pop sensibilities, there was always a nascent sweetness to Blondie that offset the naturally shy, thirtysomething Debbie's reinvention of herself as a sassy, brassy peroxide blonde. Further evidence of New York punk's feminisation came from Talking Heads, whose Tina Weymouth was a diminutive young blonde who laid down solid white funk basslines. The centre of attention though was frontman and songwriter David Byrne, a clean-cut preppie type whose ironically observed songs of modern dislocation were more danceable than anything else on the CBGB's scene.

They were art-rock, as opposed to Blondie's pop, the Ramones' thrash and Patti Smith's/Television's neo-psychedelia. The only criteria they shared is that they were no seasoned virtuosos, and they were looking to create a niche for themselves which had nothing to do with the now complacent hippie generation that went before. There was no handy, catch-all umbrella term to express this eclectic vanguard, so music press commentators fell back on the term that came courtesy of *Nuggets*, John Holmstrom, et al: 'Punk'.

1

CHAPTER 2
ORIGINAL UK PUNK

UK punk, unlike its American forebear, was visually recognisable as a movement. Johnny Rotten, the most readily identifiable icon of the era, may have disclaimed all association with anything under the nominal label 'punk' – but then, the Pistols had the privilege of having got there first. The momentum toward minimalist garage rock had been building all over the westernised world, from New York City (the Ramones – see Chapter One) to Brisbane, Australia (the Saints – see Chapter Seven). Its simultaneous eruption came from profoundly pissed-off young men, completely disaffected by what then constituted the music scene (if not by life itself).

Visually speaking, the Pistols were a combination of improvised street chic and the contrived outrage of McLaren and Westwood's Sex/Seditionaries shop designs. (Motto: 'For soldiers, prostitutes, dykes and punks.') Compare Rotten/Lydon's drape jacket held

'New Rose' by The Damned (1) – the first UK single release by an original punk band. Stiff Records were first out of the starting gate in October 1976, though many of their signings were old pub rockers.

together with safety pins or, later, Sid Vicious wearing the infamous 'cowboys' t-shirt, from a design by gay artist Tom of Finland, with Steve Jones' black PVC strides and crepe-sole shoes. It's difficult to imagine now just how startling it was for someone to wear tight drainpipe jeans and short razorcut hair, maybe with a peroxide stripe, back at the fag end of sloppy hippiedom. But it was these stylistic touches, as much as anything else, that pegged someone as a punk rocker back in 1976. (Or as 'queer' – which, while we tend to remember the more brutal elements of punk, was perhaps a natural hangover from the original Brit punks hanging out in gay clubs and copping a little of the clientele's style.)

With the exception of genuine individualists like Siouxsie, most punk band members looked more conventionally street-sharp than the walking caricatures of second and third-generation punk (no tartan bondage trousers or multicoloured Mohawks). And these elements were reflected in the record packaging of legions of post-Pistols punk bands – starting with The Damned, at the forefront of the second wave of

1

punk bands, but still coming across as cartoon characters, lining up in their PVC jackets and new haircuts to give the camera their best stare.

But the originators were on an entirely different tack. Though the original pressing of the era-defining 'Anarchy In The UK' (1976) simply looked like any old seven-inch on the EMI label, by the time the much hired-and-fired Pistols had landed with their third record label (Virgin), their perverse corporate identity had already formed. Adhering to manager McLaren and designer Jamie Reid's admiration/nostalgia for the tactics of the Marxist Situationists in the radical late 1960s, plastering the Pistols' all-too-recognisable faces all over the covers seemed very far from the point.

As Reid later put it, 'you use the same tactics that you know are going to get thrown back in your face from the likes of the *Mirror* and the *Sun*.' In fact he cannibalised the tabloid response to the cultural advent of the Pistols, with a montage of headlines like 'The Filth and the Fury', following their brief outburst of swearing on Thames TV's *Today*. From thereon, his graphic design style was an integral part of the Pistols' identity. Stealing and subverting images from official royal portraits, newspapers and holiday brochures, it attacked the sensibilities of a complacent, decaying Britain which, were it not for occasional upsurges of energy like the punk movement, would soon have become moribund.

The Clash, the second of the great Brit punk bands, shared more influences with arch-rivals the Pistols than the latter would acknowledge. Foremost among these was the influence of Situationism – this time filtered through the perspective of Clash manager Bernie Rhodes, an old acolyte of McLaren. While The Clash were seen as urgently political, as opposed to the

2

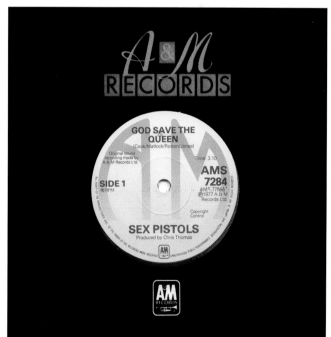

The original 1976 EMI release of 'Anarchy In The UK' was without a picture sleeve; its release in France by Virgin, seven months later, carried the almost obligatory safety pin design (2). Jamie Reid's 1977 bricollage sleeve design for Virgin's release of 'God Save The Queen' (1) has become an icon in itself, exhibited at the ICA. Its rarity is eclipsed by the song's original A&M 45 release (3), quickly withdrawn when A&M parted ways with the Pistols.

3

1

2

3

4

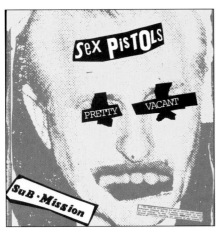

5

6

In 1977, Sex Pistols designer Jamie Reid brought the influence of Situationism to bear on the UK and US editions of 'Pretty Vacant' (1 & 2) and 'Holidays In The Sun' (7) – the original edition of 'Holidays' was withdrawn when a Belgian travel company objected to Reid subverting images from their brochure. The 1978 pic sleeves for 'No One Is Innocent' (3), 'Something Else' (4) and 'Silly Thing' (5) were all taken from the Great Rock 'N' Roll Swindle movie, an endless source of recyclable material. Reid's 1979 design for 'C'mon Everybody' (6) had less impact than his classic early Pistols work.

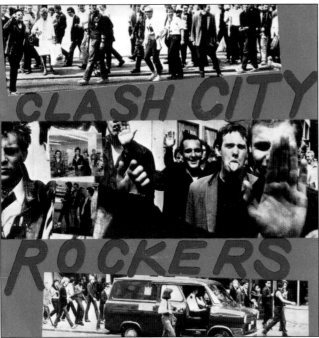

Pistols' sneering nihilism, it was rare to hear them make a direct political statement in their early days. ('Hate and War' and 'White Riot', as slogans, had all the force of a screaming police siren, but were no more inherently political than the Pistols promising, 'No future,' or co-opting the term 'anarchy'.)

But the visual impact of their sloganeering was always paramount. Whether stencilled on their jump-suits in the early days, or represented by a stage back-drop of rioting at the Notting Hill Carnival, the Britain represented by The Clash was just as absurdly hope-less as that depicted in Rotten's lyrics – but it was also a pressure cooker, things were ready to blow, and the hope existed that some people just might fight back. This apocalyptic urgency manifested on the pic sleeves of their early singles, doing much to earn them the 'political' epithet.

Of the first generation of Brit punk bands, the Buzzcocks took the opposite road to The Clash. Spikily energetic, they moved from the borderline nihilism of original singer Howard Devoto's 'Boredom' into the terrain of sexual politics, via the bittersweet love songs of new mainman Pete Shelley. They also developed a unique little corporate identity that kept their personable everyman faces off the cov-ers of their single sleeves. Instead, they favoured pas-tel-coloured geometrical designs by Malcolm Garrett, each being uniquely identifiable as a Buzzcocks release, even subverting the corporate identity of their label by utilising the UA logo. They also seemed to grow more minimalist each time although the Linder

Issued in 1977, the first Clash single, 'White Riot' (1) had an air of imminent violence. The original three members, Joe Strummer, Mick Jones and Paul Simonon, had the single's titles sprayed on their jumpsuits, with Jones showcasing a line from the B-side, '1977' ('sten guns in Knightsbridge'). 1978's 'Clash City Rockers' (2) had the same street appeal, with its images of punks and police vans, but 'Tommy Gun' (3), released later that same year, widened their apocalyptic outlook to present a more global perspective. Presciently, from a contemporary perspective, it carries Arabic script on the cover.

3

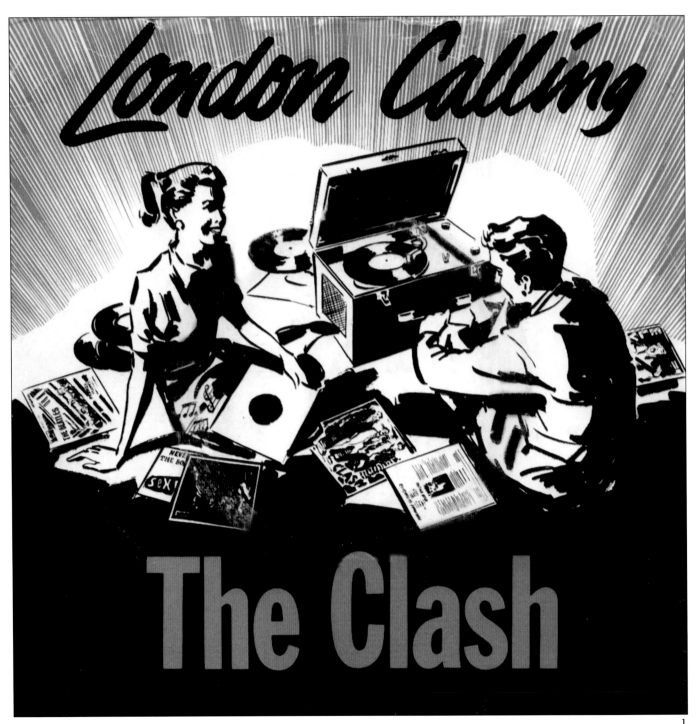

2

In the late 1970s, as their recorded output became increasingly sophisticated, The Clash's pic sleeves abandoned brute literalism. NME cartoonist Ray Lowry's 1979 sleeve for 'London Calling' (1) brings an ironic perspective to late 1950s/early 1960s pop kids spinning discs on their Dansette – placing the first Pistols and Clash albums alongside classic releases by Elvis, the Beatles and Bob Dylan. 1978's 'English Civil War' (2) uses a still from the animated film of Animal Farm, where Benjamin the donkey eyes the new pig ruling class with scepticism. Released in 1979, on the day Margaret Thatcher came to power, The Cost Of Living EP (3) subverts commercial advertising, closely mimicking the brand identity of Daz soap powder.

3

1

2

Dismissed by po-faced members of the original punk scene, The Damned endured for decades via their sense of irreverent fun. There was always a whiff of music hall theatre about them, as demonstrated by their second single, 1977's 'Neat Neat Neat' (1), and the first anniversary giveaway 'Stretcher Case' (3), with its sleeve fore-shadowing the later Goth movement. They broke up and reformed regular-ly, the cover of 'Problem Child' (2) showcasing new guitarist Lu Edmonds alongside original members Captain Sensible and Brian James. Overleaf: In 1979, the reformed Damned recorded their first singles in more than a year: 'Love Song' had four different Waldo's Design sleeves – each featuring a member of the band. Displayed here: vocalist Dave Vanian (1), guitarist Sensible (2) and drummer Rat Scabies (3). The fourth sleeve featured short-lived bassist Algy Ward. 'Smash It Up' (5) became a new anthem for teenage vandalism, while 'I Just Can't Be Happy Today' (4) fea-tured a scowling Beet-hoven bust on the front sleeve and the grinning band on the reverse both designed by Phil Smee at Waldo's Design.

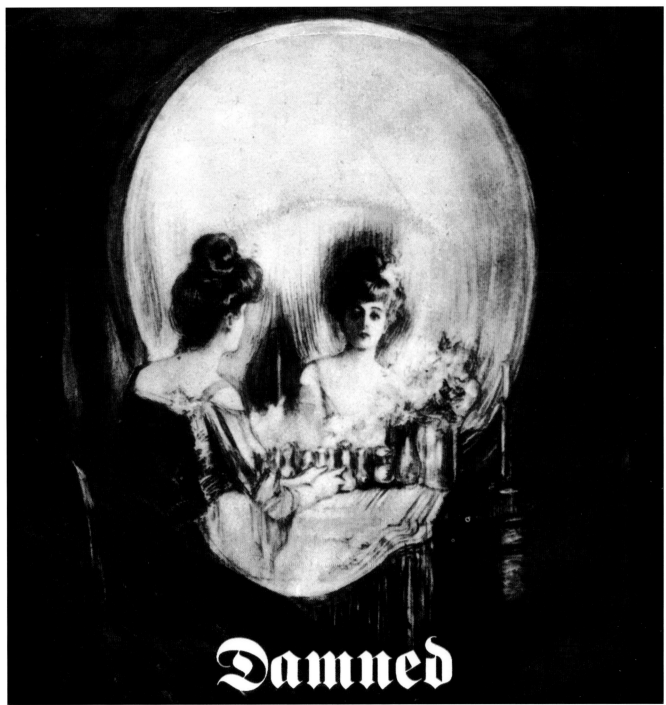

1

3

2

4

The Damned

Smash it up

PUNK ON 45

Spiral Scratch (2), the Buzzcocks' 1977 debut EP on indie label New Hormones, set the template for punk rock pic sleeves: stark typography, cheap b/w Polaroid image, group shot of band. With the departure of original vocalist Howard Devoto (far right of pic), Pete Shelley (second right) became the leader, and the Mancunian quartet became purveyors of spiky modern love songs. Their second single, 1977's 'Orgasm Addict' (1), a Devoto/Shelley song, urgently evoked adolescent sexual compulsion. Its design was by Malcolm Garrett, iconic cover collage by Linder Sterling, later of Ludus, then Devoto's partner. Assembled from pornography, women's magazines and the Argos catalogue, it's hard to dislodge from the mind. The Buzzcocks design, typography and nifty corporate logo from Orgasm Addict onward were by designer Malcolm Garrett. As he says of his pic sleeves, 'I saw it as a piece of cardboard which was an expression of the mood that is Buzzcocks. I didn't want it to be like a punk sleeve. Handwritten stuff and torn paper was already a cliché. I hit on the idea that each sleeve should be done in two colours' (3). Each subsequent single (1-7) appears on the following two pages.

2

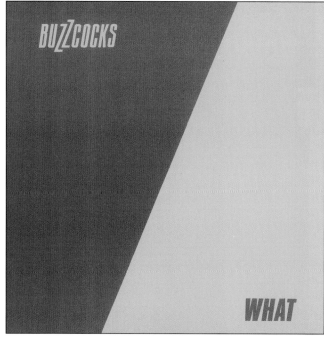

3

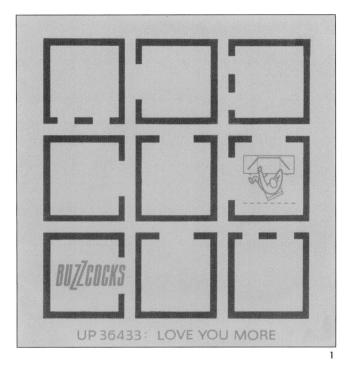

1

3

2

4

Stirling cover, the garishly antisexual collage of 'Orgasm Addict', had an abiding influence on punk visuals, with its clash of glaring pornographic images and household consumer items.

Siouxsie and the Banshees, whose 1976 debut gig featured a bang-crashing Sid Vicious on drums, were ostensibly among the original UK punks. By the time of their 1978 debut release, 'Hong Kong Garden', line-up changes and the space to develop a unique style (which, imitated with less flair and imagination, would later be termed 'Gothic') had made them a very distinct entity indeed. Initially, record labels had been wary of the Banshees due to Siouxsie's *Cabaret*-style flouting of the Nazi swastika, and a perceived flirtation with similar taboos in their lyrics. But it became clear that the Banshees had no political agenda, and that theirs was an internal world of personal psychosis and suburban relapses. Their early single covers, too, represented this, redolent of the most psychologically disturbing works of filmmaker Roman Polanski, a personal favourite of Siouxsie. (Though she once heartlessly dedicated their cover of the Beatles' 'Helter Skelter' to Polanski. The song was a favourite of the Manson Family, who murdered his pregnant wife.)

Other early Brit punk bands featured confound the lazy stereotypes as to what punk actually *was*. The underrated Subway Sect seem, with

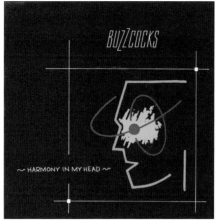

5

6

7

Pages 50-51: From 1978, when Siouxsie and the Banshees signed a long overdue recording contract with Polydor, their covers epitomised the Gothic aesthetic – before the term was ever applied to rock music. 'Hong Kong Garden' (1) features an image resembling Polanski's The Tenant *or Franju's* Eyes Without a Face – *though the kitsch cartoon on the Japanese edition (2) makes Siouxsie look like Magenta in* The Rocky Horror Show. *The noirish intrigue of 'The Staircase (Mystery)' (3) resembles a scene from* The Third Man. *'Mittageisen' (4), while harshly metallic in its sound, is a tribute to German anti-Nazi propagandist John Heartfield. His photomontage of the same name satirised the Third Reich's 'guns, not butter' philosophy – as a record cover, it's an effective response to hysterical allegations of the Banshees harbouring Nazi sympathies. 1979's sinister 'Playground Twist' (5) features original cover art, painted by a disabled child.*

1

2

3

4

5

hindsight, to have been oddly diffident compared to the filth and the fury going on all around them. But vocalist Vic Godard's lyrics were probably the most intelligent to come out of the early punk scene, with an elliptical perceptiveness and gift for wordplay way beyond most other garage bands. The Slits, too, were adept at overturning expectations. Standard bearers for the dogma that said punk women were no longer defined by sex, these fiercely vital young viragos were, at first, either loved or hated for their shambolic, half-shouted/half-shrieked performances. By the time their personal anthem, 'Typical Girls', was released as a single in 1979, they had a little more dubwise light and space in their sound, courtesy of reggae producer Dennis Bovell.

Few of these bands jibe with any kind of punk rock stereotype – but as far as the UK goes, they were the originals. Their one unifying factor was the defiant belief that they could get up and do it, with no apologies to the elitist hippie music industry. Most were as far from the clanging dole queue/high rise/1977 punk orthodoxy (based on the Pistols/Clash template, but lacking the originality and imagination) as it was possible for a 1970s Brit garage band to be. The ''77 shit pile' would follow soon enough.

1

2

Atypical punks: Before 'punk' became a straitjacket, Subway Sect presented singer Vic Godard's elliptical view of modern life. 'Nobody's Scared' (1) was released the year after its 1977 recording; its single sleeve is a pre-Photoshop cut-and-paste of the band sitting on the lines as a WWII-era tube train approaches. 'Ambition' (2) was the poppy second single by this almost forgotten band, the pic sleeve showing Godard leaving a train station. All-girl punk pioneers the Slits were a long time in getting their signature tunes to vinyl too: 'Typical Girls' (3) finally saw release by Island in 1979 – by which time its discordant element was smoothed out by Dennis Bovell's dubwise production, and the band were captured in feral dayglo by Island art director Dennis Morris.

1

CHAPTER 3

THE SECOND WAVE OF UK PUNK

And so it was that Western pop culture was laid waste by a great tidal wave known as 'Punk', and all that came before Year Zero (i.e. 1976) was swept away . . .

Except that it wasn't quite like that. Though it's easy to view the era with phlegm-soaked nostalgia, it's as well to remember that, when the Pistols were granted their first *Top of the Pops* video appearance with 'Pretty Vacant' (their third single) in 1977, family-friendly MOR acts like Abba and the Brotherhood of Man still topped the charts.

Certainly though, in (once Great) Britain, any young band who dispensed with flared jeans, stuck a safety pin through a skinny tie and sang very fast and aggressively about life on the dole, or a notorious murderer, or (at a push) their girlfriend would meet the playground definition of 'punk'. Punk was also midwife to the overnight birth of a cottage industry. After initial innovators like Stiff (who predated punk slightly, but

'Your Generation' (1) by Generation X – a 1977 modernist design, via way of Mondrian and Le Corbusier, for a band in thrall to the pop art of the 1960s.

released The Damned's 'New Rose') and Step Forward came a whole plethora of small labels – some of which encouraged DIY creativity and expanded way beyond the slew of guttural Pistols/Clash imitators, others of which exhibited no discernment or originality at all.

Many other artists featured in this section signed to major labels, anxious to stake out their corner of the emergent punk/'new wave' market – as with the fore-runners of the scene, the Pistols (EMI/A&M/Virgin) and The Clash (CBS). Generation X (signed to Chrysalis) were pop-art-painted pretty boys, whose songwriting team of Billy Idol and Tony James had decamped from early punk band Chelsea, which strident but one-dimensional vocalist Gene October would keep going with identipunk songs about the dole and tower blocks. (James had also been a member of London SS, the seminal but hypothetical band that featured Mick Jones, later of The Clash, and future Damned guitarist Brian James, but never actually played anywhere.)

Gen X's opening salvo, 'Your Generation', was a sardonic riff on The Who's 'My Generation', paying lip service to the dogma which held that all 1960s rock

1

3

4

2

5

In Japan, where the kids took to Generation X's pretty-boy power-pop in a big way, their pic sleeves for 'Your Generation' (1), 'Wild Youth' (3) and 'Ready Steady Go' (5) replaced the 1960s pop-art influence of the original designs for 1977's 'Wild Youth' (2) and '78's 'Ready Steady Go' (4).

Billy Idol and Tony James of Gen X decamped from the original Chelsea after three gigs, leaving vocalist Gene October to soldier on with the name. Chelsea became the first identikit punk band: 1977's 'Right To Work' (6) was exhilaratingly strident, but was followed later that year by the further nouveau-clichés of 'High Rise Living' (7). By the time of 'Urban Kids' in 1979 (8), one of the last releases on punk independent Step Forward, they wore a slap-panned glam look worthy of Gen X themselves.

7

6

8

1

Slaughter and the Dogs claimed to predate the Sex Pistols. As seen on their 1977 singles, 'Cranked Up Really High' (1) and 'Where Have All The Boot Boys Gone?' (2, Spanish edition), their 1970s lad chic was as redolent of the Faces as the punks. Despite catchy singles like 1978's 'Quick Joey Small', a cover of a 1960s US bubblegum hit (3, Spanish edition), the Mancunian hooligans never really found their niche. More successful were X-Ray Spex. After the gloriously cacophonic '77 debut 'Oh Bondage! Up Yours!' (4), they replaced original sax player Laura Logic and struck a deal with major label EMI in 1978, beginning with 'Identity' (5 Japanese edition). Vocalist Poly Styrene's love/hate fascination with artificiality found expression on the covers of 'The Day The World Turned Dayglo' (6) and 'Germ Free Adolescents' (7) – the latter utilising a mocked-up Jamie Reid-style advertising parody.

2

3

4

6

5

7

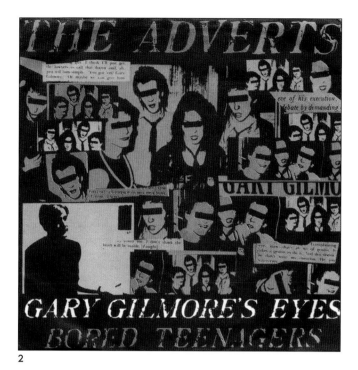

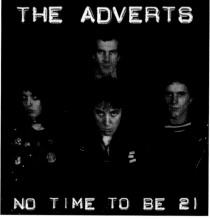

West Country band the Adverts were among the most powerful to form after seeing the Pistols, with a spurt of downbeat hits on the Anchor label. Stiff Records were smart enough to put the face of Gaye Advert on the cover of their 1977 debut 45, 'One Chord Wonders' (1). Though her role in the line-up – seen on the sleeve of 1978's 'No Time To Be 21' (5), singer T.V. Smith in the foreground – was as the bassist, she was one of the few sex symbols of the punk era. Songwriter Smith was sceptical of the 'new wave', as expressed in their 1977 single 'Safety In Numbers' (3 & 4, UK and German editions). But their sleeve designers utilised the cut-and-paste look, not least on the morbidly catchy 'Gary Gilmore's Eyes' (2) – the bands' eyes blacked out as an allusion to how US killer Gilmore (seen bottom left of pic sleeve) had pledged his eyes to medical science after his execution.

1

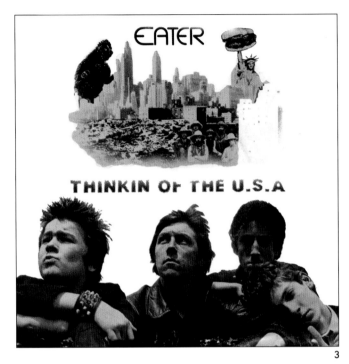

3

2

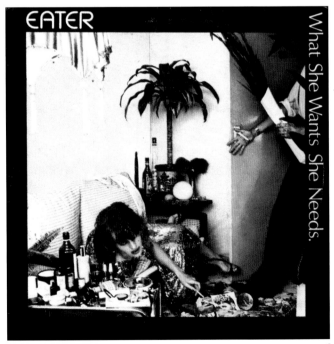

4

5

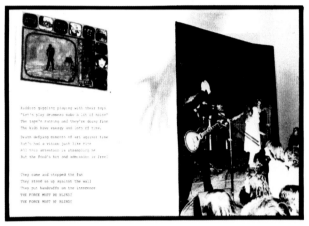

7

ALTERNATIVE TV

6

Eater were 1977's junior punks, seen in the secondary school uniforms of 'Outside View' (1). Singer Andy Blade was fifteen, while drummer Dee Generate (foreground of pic sleeve) was even younger. Formed in late 1976, they were popular enough to release a second single 'Lock It Up' (2) in punk-hungry Japan. The cover of 1978's 'Thinkin' Of The USA' (3) reduces America to clichés of NYC, hamburgers, pioneers – and Godzilla (who's Japanese); 'What She Wants She Needs' (4) glamorises rock'n'roll excess, something punk never fully eschewed. Much more radical were Alternative TV: Mark P, editor/publisher of Sniffin' Glue fanzine, had a wide musical palette that rejected punk orthodoxy – as seen in a record collection that includes Kim Fowley's Outrageous LP, on the cover of their '77 debut 'How Much Longer' (5), and the Sound City reggae/dance music emporium on 'Life After Life' (6), released the following year. By the time of 1979's 'The Force Is Blind' (7), ATV incorporated low-tech variations on dub, psychedelia and ambient music.

1

9

The Mekons were named after the alien in UK comic strip Dan Dare – Pilot of the Future. Formed by art students at Leeds University, their 1977 debut, 'Never Been In A Riot' (1), was close to the rama-lama punk it parodied. Greater things were promised by 1978's 'Where Were You?' (2), whose clanging repetition spoke of their future experimentalism.

3

4

The Boys were a more
conventional powerpop
band; their 1977 single
cover for 'First Time' (3)
may have spoken of
high-rise punk clichés,
but it was a rough-edged
love song – as was
1978's 'Brickfield Nights'
(4), with its intriguing
faceless cover model. The
Boys established a
tradition of recording dire
Christmas singles as 'the
Yobs' – like 'Rub-A-Dum-
Dum' (5) in 1979, their
version of 'Little
Drummer Boy'. The Nazi
uniform is a hamfisted
reference to their cover
of 'Run Rudolph Run',
which featured Rudolf
Hess on the sleeve.

4

2

5

999 featured two Londoners who might have been pub/punk rock also-rans: vocalist Nick Cash, formerly of Kilburn and the High Roads, and Pablo LaBritain, who briefly rehearsed as drummer for The Clash. Released in 1977, their first United Artists single, 'Nasty! Nasty!' (1), was a shout-along bandwagon jumper, as in-your-face as its pic sleeve. But from thereon 999 grew more melodic, having minor or near pop-punk hits in 1978 with 'Emergency' (2, Japanese version), 'Me And My Desire' (3), 'Feelin' Alright With The Crew' (4), and in 1979 with 'Homicide' (5), 'I'm Alive' (6) and 'Found Out Too Late' (7).

3

6

4

7

1

4

2

5

3

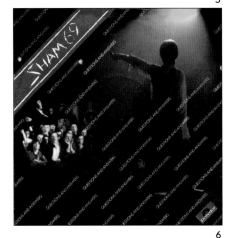

6

Hailing from Hersham in leafy Surrey, Sham 69 were the unlikeliest 'cockney cowboys'. But for a while they were the great working-class hopes of punk. (Although vocalist Jimmy Pursey, left on the cover of 1978's 'Angels With Dirty Faces' (7), was later revealed as privately educated, unlike the masses he claimed to speak for.) Beginning with their 1977 Step Forward debut, 'I Don't Wanna' (1), their second slice of inarticulate angst was 1978's 'Borstal Breakout' (2), a chant about the youth custody system for major label Polydor. The populist approach paid, and hits followed: 'If The Kids Are United' (3) was a sentimental stomp-along; 'Hurry Up, Harry' (4 & 5, UK and Japanese editions) was a moronic knees-up, its cover evoking dull 1970s pubs and bad beer. By the time of 1979's 'Questions And Answers' (6), Sham were increasingly irrelevant – bedevilled by far-right skinheads among their following and out-brutalised by the nascent 'oi!' bands.

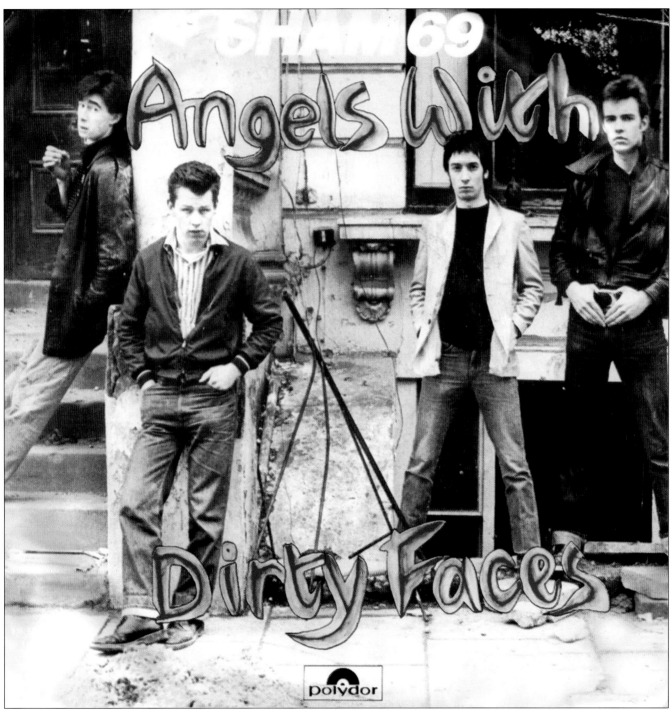

1

2

3

4

One of the last of the 1977 Roxy bands, the U.K. Subs were keepers of the flame for those who liked punk rock fast, fierce and ragged. Whether they were singing about the police on their 1978 debut 'C.I.D.' (4), punk love on their 1979 hit 'Stranglehold' (1 & 5, UK and Spanish editions – enigmatic cover image taken from the Subs' debut LP) or 'Tomorrow's Girls' (2) or covering the Zombies' 1960s classic 'She's Not There' (3), they were always a noise riot.

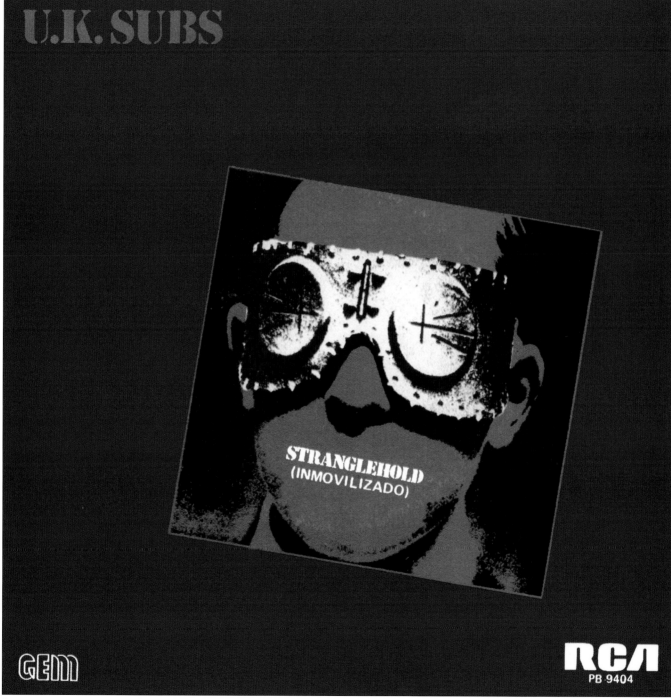

stars were boring old farts who needed to be swept away. But by the time of 'Ready Steady Go' (which namechecked the Beatles, the Stones and Cathy McGowan, hostess of the eponymous pop TV show), it was clear that all they wanted was to be famous pop stars themselves.

X-Ray Spex were a much more interesting shade of dayglo. Led by young Londoner Marion Elliott, who restyled herself as Poly Styrene and wore braces on her teeth, her songs and their exhilaratingly cacophonous sax player broke the already conventional punk-band mould. Signed (perhaps ironically) by the giant EMI corporation, Ms Styrene's lyrics were hallucinatory love-hate tributes to the consumer society such as 'The Day The World Turned Dayglo'. But by the time of their final hit, 'Germ Free Adolescents', Poly had rejected all the artificial tack in her life after experiencing a vision of a visiting spacecraft.

Similarly extraterrestrial, but in a purely cartoonish way, Scottish band the Rezillos boasted a singer, Fay Fife, who was like a 1960s mod-mutant reborn for the punk age. Their biggest hit, 'Top Of The Pops', celebrated the tacky glitz of the UK pop chart show in the same way Gen X lionised 'Ready Steady Go'.

Also making occasional assaults upon the charts in 1977-8, the Adverts were a vehicle for the pessimistic vision of singer-song-

1

2

3

Rama-lama-lama-one-two-three-four! Identikit punk in stark pic sleeves: Menace were shouty punk at its shoutiest, on 1977's 'Screwed Up' (1) and the following year's 'G.L.C.' (2). The latter chanted out that the Greater London Council was 'full of shit', before Labour politician Ken Livingstone took over the running and it became trendy to defend the G.L.C. against Margaret Thatcher. 'Runnin' Riot' by Cock Sparrer (3, Spanish edition) was a 1977 blueprint for the 'oi!' punk of the early 1980s; aggressive football-hooligan rock.

writer T.V. Smith. They also featured panda-eyed bassist Gaye Advert, who, along with Fay Fife, was one of UK punk's very few sex symbols. (One of the aspects of early punk was its asexuality, aided by speed as its drug of choice.) While the first of the Adverts' rapid string of hits, 'Gary Gilmore's Eyes', was a horror-comic shaggy dog yarn about the recently executed killer, 'Safety In Numbers' was a jangling lament for the 'new wave', mourning the loss of the individualism briefly inherent in punk.

Not all of UK punk was disappearing up a one-dimensional dead end, however. Mark P(erry), editor of the seminal *Sniffin' Glue* fanzine, continued to eschew conformity with his band Alternative TV – as much influenced by dub reggae and Frank Zappa as any of the aggressive guitar bands that catalysed punk. The Mekons' debut, 'Never Been In A Riot', appeared in 1977 on Fast Records (Bob Last's seminal indie label, also home to classic post-punk band the Gang of Four), and had much in common with the prevailing school of rama-lama three-chord punk. The clanging repetition of its follow-up, 'Where Were You?', however, suggested a penchant for experiment which they would develop through the subsequent decades – including a celebrated cross-pollination with US country music.

Maverick solo acts with idiosyncratic lyrics met with varying degrees of success: Patrik Fitzgerald held the distinction of being Britain's first folk-punk singer, recording with an acoustic guitar for the Small Wonder label; the plucky east Londoner became renowned on the punk circuit for having full beer cans hurled at him as missiles from the audience. Mancunian punk poet John Cooper Clarke fared better, partly due to possessing the stagecraft of a raconteur-comedian. Signed to CBS, his jokey mix of grimy realism and grotesque whimsy, set to the cinematic soundtrack of the Invisible Girls (who included Joy Division producer Martin Hannett), failed to set the charts alight, but granted him a degree of longevity. (His career would take him through the highs and lows of heroin addiction and also team him with the Honey Monster for a Sugar Puffs ad.)

But for most of its audience, punk became a rigid genre that provided little scope for progression. For every group like Penetration – whose charismatic Pauline Murray sang Patti Smith's 'Free Money', and whose dual guitarists were seemingly inspired by Tom Verlaine and Richard Lloyd of Television – there were now dozens of identipunk bands who adhered to the template of speed, aggression, and little else. Enjoying scant commercial success, their almost forgotten single releases have become collector's items by default – in some cases they may be classics of their kind, but for the most part they simply evoke their own era, and the cheap visual appeal of the now generic picture sleeve.

Most endearing of this abrasive bunch were Slaughter and the Dogs. Heavily influenced by glam-era Bowie/the Spiders from Mars, this Mancunian four-some boasted that they were blaring out garage rock before the Sex Pistols had even formed. Resembling the sharper-dressed kind of 1970s football hooligan, by the time they issued their debut single, 'Cranked Up Really High', they really did sound like the kind of speed-freak punks the song evoked.

By this time, 1977's 'Summer of Hate', punk had long since transcended its London roots. Beginning with the Buzzcocks in Manchester, who formed immediately after witnessing one of the Pistols' earliest Northern gigs, all major (and some minor) UK cities now had their own local punk scene. It was almost like a collision between the parochialism of early 1960s Merseybeat and the rawer R&B beat boom that swept the country afterwards. While only a handful of the second-generation bands displayed any real verve or creativity, it was nonetheless a stepping stone for performers who later came to the fore – and might have remained in total obscurity if not for the energising force of punk.

Riff Raff were from the east London suburb of Barking, touring for two years before they dissolved and vocalist/guitarist Billy Bragg joined the army; north London's the Nipple Erectors (later the Nips)

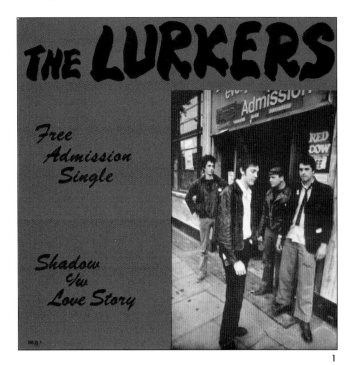

1

2

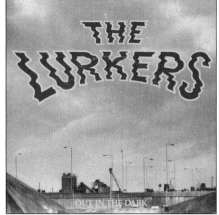

3

4

5

The Lurkers were Ickenham, Middlesex's answer to the Ramones – fast, furious, and not very serious. 'Shadow' (1), their 1977 debut on the Beggars Banquet label, allowed free admission to a gig at their regular venue, the Red Cow pub. 'Freak Show' (2), the ultimate nightmare date song, featured a pic sleeve by legendary cartoonist Savage Pencil. 'Ain't Got A Clue' (3), 'Out In The Dark' (4) and 'New Guitar In Town' (5) followed in 1978-9.

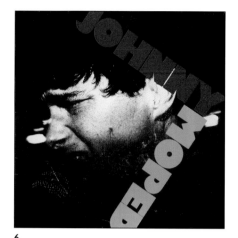

6

7

10

More fun-punk: Johnny Moped was from Croydon's pub scene, and a friend of The Damned's Captain Sensible. Although everything about him — including the anti-hip parody of motorcycle culture inherent in his name — seemed to mock rock'n'roll, he could lay down some blistering singles such as 1977's 'Incendiary Device' (6). 1978 follow ups 'Darling Let's Have Another Baby' (7) and 'Little Queenie' (8) were released by pub-rock pioneers Chiswick. The second of the three contained a creditable cover of Eddie Cochran's 'Something Else' (prior to the Sid Vicious version) on its B-side. Scots band the Rezillos were the fun elements of 1960s pop filtered through the day-glo trash aesthetic. In their string of minor hits for the Sire label, cartoonish vocalists Fay Fife and Eugene Reynolds owed as much to The Jetsons as the Ramones. Pictured here are 1977's '(My Baby Does) Good Sculptures' (9) and 'Cold Wars' (10), and 1978's 'Top Of The Pops' (11) and 'Destination Venus' (12).

8

11

9

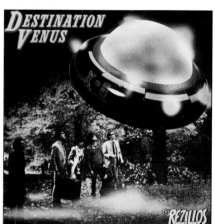

12

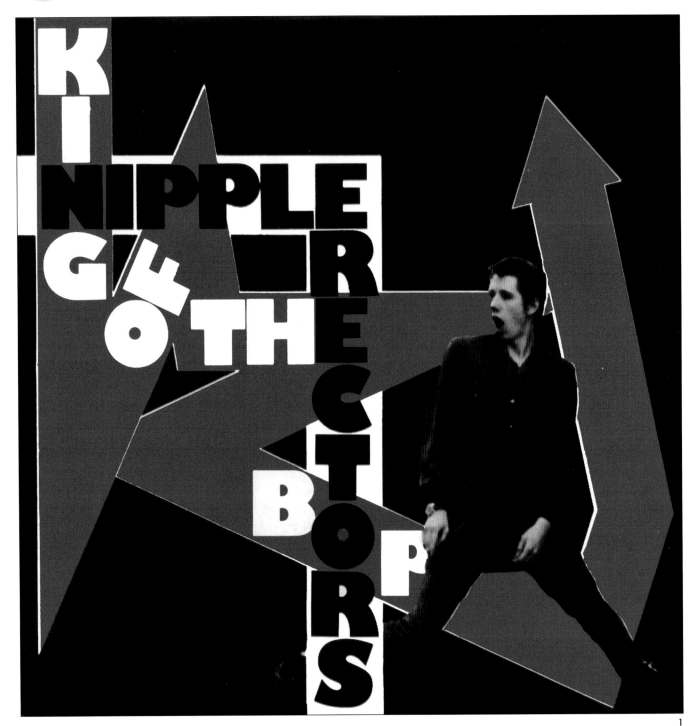

1

2

Who said there's no future? Alternative and mainstream performers of the 1980s were showcased in these independent punk singles: Shane O'Hooligan, vocalist of the rockabilly-tinged Nipple Erectors, is unmistakable on their 1978 debut 'King Of The Bop' (1), although he's less distinct on the following year's 'Gabrielle' (2) — by which point the band had moderated their name to the Nips — and is clearly Shane MacGowan of the Pogues; 1977's 'Johnny Won't Get To Heaven' (3) by the Killjoys has a surreal perspective to its cover design, considering it's just a shout-along tribute to (supposedly) Johnny Rotten — sung by young Brummie Kevin Rowland, who later got soul with Dexy's Midnight Runners.

3

1

2

3

*More alternative and mainstream performers of the 1980s: Johnny
& the Self Abusers had changed their name to Simple Minds by the
time Chiswick issued 'Saints And Sinners' (3) in 1977; 1978 single 'I
Wanna Be A Cosmonaut' (1) by Riff Raff featured the dulcet tones
of Billy Bragg, the Bard of Barking; the same year, Demon Preacher,
later reconstituted as Alien Sex Fiend, got sleazy with 'Little Miss
Perfect' (2) – the cover girl was Joyce McKinney, who excited the
tabloids in '77 by abducting a young Mormon missionary and
forcing him to engage in 'sex in chains' (or ropes, she claims); Big In
Japan's posthumous 1978 From Y To Z And Never Again EP (4)
features the frighteningly striking Jayne Casey on the cover, later of
Pink Industry/Pink Military – her better-known ex-bandmates include
Holly Johnson of Frankie Goes To Hollywood, Bill Drummond of the
KLF, Ian Broudie of the Lightning Seeds and Budgie of the Banshees.*

4

Revolutions on Vinyl

1

3

2

Punk soon hit 'the provinces' in 1976/77, catalysing the
Radiators From Space in Dublin. Their April 1977 debut, 'Television
Screen' (1) was a rama-lama rant, while 'Sunday World' (2) Irish release
only sniped at redtop tabloids. Vocalist/guitarist Philip Chevron's lyrics
flowered with the truncation of the band name to 'the Radiators':
1979's 'Let's Talk About The Weather' (3) was a surprisingly tender
punk love song. But Chevron would find greater success with the
Pogues. In the North of Ireland, Rudi gave the Undertones a run for
their money with 1978's catchy 'Big Time' (4) – though why the sleeve
used a still from 1930s horror movie The Mummy's Hand is unclear.
In Newcastle, Penetration, named after the Iggy and the Stooges song,
featured charismatic vocalist Pauline Murray; Virgin releases like their
1977 debut 'Don't Dictate' (5), and 1978-9 follow ups 'Firing Squad'
(6), 'Life's A Gamble' (7) and 'Come Into The Open' (8) were lyrically
banal, but redeemed by Murray's delivery and some dual guitar
interplay. When Penetration split, she briefly found expression with
the more experimental Invisible Girls, onetime backing band of
John Cooper Clarke.

4

6

7

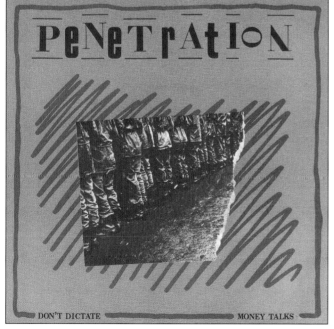

5

8

were rockabilly-tinged punks featuring vocalist Shane O'Hooligan, a London Irishman notorious for wearing a Union Jack jacket (at a gig by The Jam, who fetishised the Union flag) and getting his ear sliced open at an early Clash gig. Both young men would embrace the roots of, respectively, English and Irish folk music in the 1980s, combined with the ramshackle dynamics of punk-Shane reverting to his real surname of MacGowan to form classic punk-folk band the Pogues.

In Dublin, the Radiators from Space (later just 'the Radiators') followed their standard rama-lama debut 'Television Screen' with more thoughtful songs like 'Kitty Ricketts' (a kind of Irish 'Lili Marleen'), showcasing the talents of songwriter Phil Chevron. When the Radiators split without success, migrating to London would bring him into contact with Shane MacGowan, and earn him a pivotal role in the Pogues. In Liverpool, the house punk band at Eric's Club, Big In Japan, were a future scouse talent stable. Striking vocalist Jayne Casey became a mainstay of art-punks Pink Military/Pink Industry, but was outstripped in terms of fame by her bandmates: Bill Drummond went on to join The Teardrop Explodes and form the KLF, notoriously cremating £1 million on the isle of Jura; Ian Broudie, latterly of the Lightning Seeds, would be responsible for the England football squad anthem 'Three Lions'; Holly Johnson became the lead singer of Frankie Goes To Hollywood, while drummer Budgie briefly became the only male in the Slits before partnering up with Siouxsie in the Banshees.

In Birmingham, the hollering vocalist of the Killjoys was future Celtic soul brother Kevin Rowland, of Dexy's Midnight Runners; Glasgow's Johnny & the Self Abusers swiftly transformed into the Bowie/Roxy Music-influenced Simple Minds, just in time for the electronic 'neu musick' bandwagon (latter reinventing themselves again as stadium rockers). And back in the Smoke, dark-tinged punk band Demon Preacher would transform themselves by cartoonish degree into Alien Sex Fiend, big-haired stars of early Goth club the Batcave.

Out of all the many second-generation punk bands – like the Lurkers, who were Fulham, London SW15's answer to the Ramones, or Eater, who boasted of being the youngest punks on the circuit and played a cover of Alice Cooper's 'I'm Eighteen' (called 'I'm Fifteen') – few reduced the identipunk ethos to its essence as brutally as Sham 69. First recorded by Miles Copeland's independent Step Forward, their signing by Polydor inaugurated a new school of populist punk. Sham were what many people claimed punk was supposed to be: working class, earnest and (sometimes woefully) inarticulate.

Beetle-browed vocalist Jimmy Pursey had an idiotic charisma that appealed to the nascent skinhead revival – working class youth who rejected the artistic experimentalism of the more left-field bands. (Along with any hint of effeminacy or, very often, racial tolerance – a liking for reggae being by now a punk, rather than skinhead, tradition.) Songs like 'Borstal Breakout' and 'Angels With Dirty Faces' were football chant laments for 'the kids', who the emotionally overwrought Pursey (later revealed as a middle-class ex-public schoolboy) was convinced had to be 'united'. With such confused rhetoric, it's hardly surprising that Sham attracted a following of Far Right skinheads they found hard to shake off. Increasingly comical, they laid down the foundations for the shaved-skulls-and-shouting 'oi!' movement that punk rock would devolve into by the early 1980s.

1

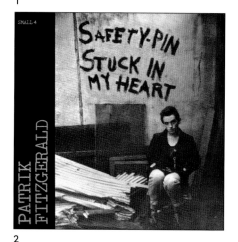

2

3

Punk could still be a sanctuary for maverick individualism. Mancunian John Cooper Clarke's 1977 Innocents EP (1) set his punk poems to a low-tech electronica backing; for 1978's 'Post-War Glamour Girl' (3), in its surrealistically kitsch pic sleeve, he was backed by the Invisible Girls, whose members included Pete Shelley of the Buzzcocks and producer Martin Hannett. Later, Cooper Clarke used his skill as a raconteur to revert to vocal performances only. Patrik Fitzgerald was just as audacious but less successful; 'Safety-Pin Stuck In My Heart' (2) showcased his punk-minstrel-with-cockney-inflexions style.

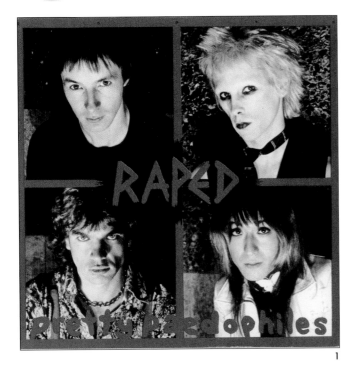

1

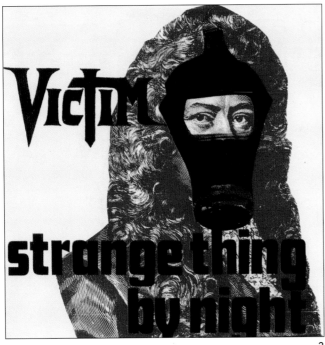

2

1977's Pearls and swine: The glam look of Raped's Pretty Paedophiles EP (1) undermined its contrived controversy, in the era when a lorry driver trashed his TV after hearing the Sex Pistols swear; today, they'd run the risk of a lynching. The 'found images' aesthetic is seen in the classifieds of the Unwanted's 'Withdrawal' (3) and the vacant-eyed punkette of 'Terminal Stupid' (7) by the Snivelling Shits, featuring Sounds' Giovanni Dadomo and future producer Steve Lillywhite. Some Chicken play moody for the cacophonous 'New Religion' (4), as do the Users with 'Sick Of You' (5). Cut-and-paste juxtaposition is used for the apocalyptic covers of Victim's 'Strange Thing By Night' (2) and 'I Am A Dalek' (6) by the Art Attacks, who featured cartoonist Savage Pencil.

3

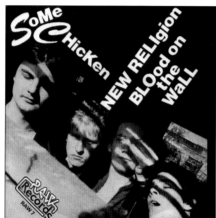

4

5

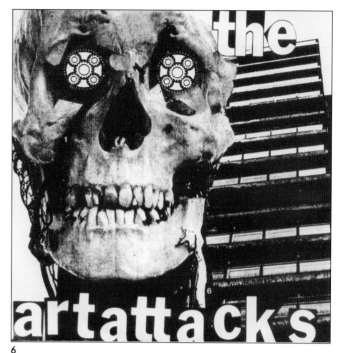

6

7

Band shots were de rigeur for the growing legions of 1977-8 identikit punks, as evidenced by the Cortinas' 'Fascist Dictator' (1), the Panik's prescient 'It Won't Sell' (2), the Drones' 'Temptations Of A White Collar Worker' (3), Cyanide's cover of The Who's 'I'm A Boy' (5) and China Street's 'You're A Ruin' (7), while powerpoppers the Stukas win 'Twats of the Year 1977' for 'Klean Living Kids' (8). The Cortinas' second and final Step Forward single 'Defiant Pose' (4) depicts Sonny puking in Mum's perfect kitchen. As with Raped, the Valves' 'Robot Love' (6) evokes glam as much as it does punk.

5

7

6

8

CHAPTER 4
NEW WAVE

'After the Pistols that term New Wave *was the kiss of death! Elvis Costello into Joe Jackson into Tom Robinson . . . . The first time I heard the term it sickened me and turned my stomach. If you settle for something so flimsy and vacuous as* New Wave, *you certainly don't deserve to buy anything I put out. I'd be appalled if that was my audience.'*

– John Lydon, *Rotten: No Irish, No Blacks, No Dogs*

Stiff Records were canny when they repackaged the cream of the pub rockers. On the 1977 'Bunch of Stiffs' tour, the rotating headliners bill comprised Nick Lowe, who recorded the first Stiff single, the sardonically poppy 'So It Goes', Wreckless Eric, who had just released a forgotten garage rock classic, 'Whole Wide World', and token hairy Larry Wallis, formerly of hippie band the Pink Fairies.

But it soon became apparent there were only two co-headlining stars: Ian Dury, formerly of Kilburn and

Released in 1977, 'Peaches' (1) reinforced the Stranglers' reputation as the dirty old men of the new wave, with the leering innuendo that the original punks found passe.

the High Roads and now well into his thirties, and the younger Declan McManus, formerly of country rock band Flip City, now re-christened Elvis Costello. Dury, a charismatically Dickensian performer with a leg wasted by polio, was already an influence on the stagecraft of a young John Lydon. But the sulphate aggression of the punks had little in common with his grimy music hall humour and the insidiously catchy white funk backing of his new band, the Blockheads. Dury quickly built up an appreciative audience of everyday Joes and Janes, as well as punks. Early Blockheads singles, from 'Sex & Drugs & Rock 'N' Roll' through the smash hit 'Hit Me With Your Rhythm Stick', are cheeky cultural remnants of late 1970s Britain – with an upbeat design aesthetic that betrays Dury's art school training under pop artist Peter Blake.

Costello was launched as a solo performer (later adding regular backing band the Attractions) with b/w press photos that made much of his innate geekiness, high forehead and spectacles. (The new wave was a godsend for the unprepossessing.) He had nothing in common with punk, his songs being vitriolic little pop

1

3

2

4

5

7

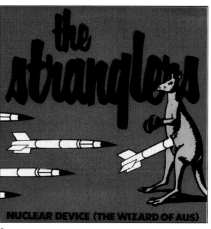

8

6

9

The Stranglers disclaimed the label 'punk rock', despite supporting both Patti Smith and the Ramones on their first UK tours. But 1977 singles 'Grip'/'London Lady'(1), 'No More Heroes' (2) and 1978's 'Something Better Change'/ 'Straighten Out' (4, US EP edition) are neo-psychedelic garage-rock classics. The band's murky aesthetic was exemplified by 'rattus norvegicus' as their emblem – as on the Spanish edition of 'No More Heroes' (3), the blistering assault of '5 Minutes' (7, Japanese edition, 1978) and the Weegee-style scene-of-crime shot on 'Nice 'N' Sleazy' (5, 1978). But melody won out over murk, and the Stranglers' softer numbers became permanent live fixtures: as with 'Walk On By' (6, French edition, 1978) – the mystery female face imposed on vocalist Hugh Cornwell is not original singer Dionne Warwick), 1979 single 'Duchess' (8) featured the band as unlikely choirboys while 'Nuclear Device' (9) took a swipe at Australian nuclear policy.

1

2

3

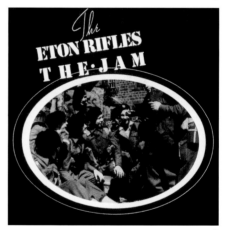

4

5

For The Jam, 'The Modern World' (1) of 1977 was the 'mod' world. The three adolescents from Surrey surfed the punk wave, but instead of destroying the past they fell in love with it: as witnessed by 'The News Of The World' (6), on which they walk down Carnaby Street, a leftover from the swinging 60s, in the famous 'Jam shoes' (two-tone brogues) and pop-art T-shirt. Songwriter Paul Weller outgrew being a mod/Who revivalist, producing observational songs from a distinctly English perspective: 1978's 'Down In The Tube Station At Midnight' (2) tells of a hapless victim beaten close to death on the London Underground; The following year's 'Strange Town' (3) gives the disorientated perspective of the young naif newly arrived in London; 'The Eton Rifles' (4) wraps the British class struggle up in a great vortex of sound. The Jam's sartorial style and 60s fetish led to an underwhelming mod revival, pre-empted by misfires like 1978's 'I Can't Wait' (5) by Scottish R&B band The Jolt.

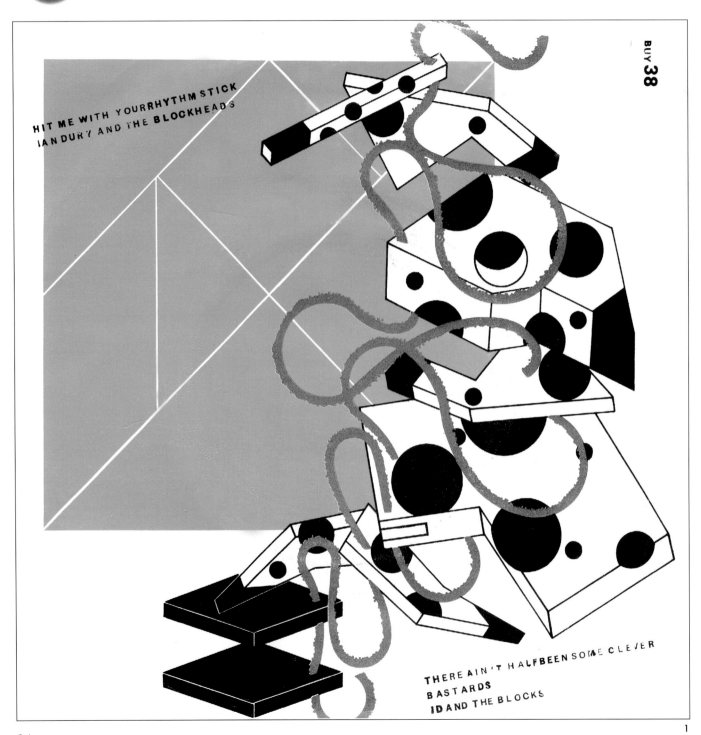

PUNK ON 45

2

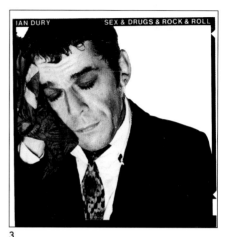

3

4

If it ain't Stiff, it ain't worth a f**k: Essex geezer Ian Dury had a uniquely British look equal parts debonair and pikey, as seen on his 1977 debut single 'Sex & Drugs & Rock 'N' Roll' (3). With the Blockheads, he became Stiff Records' major star, the white funk music hall of 1978's 'Hit Me With Your Rhythm Stick' (1) and 'What A Waste' (4) finding a place at the top of the UK charts and in the nation's heart. The graphics on the former are by Barney Bubbles, Stiff's corporate designer, and relate more directly to the B-side, 'There Ain't Half Been Some Clever Bastards' – flip the cover, and the geometric design is assembled into a spotty dog. Former Stiff labelmates Elvis Costello and the Attractions decamped to co-director Jake Riviera's new label, Radar Records – their short-lived design style also originated by Bubbles. Costello's acerbic pop vignettes of the time are represented here by '(I Don't Want To Go To) Chelsea' (2) and 'Radio Radio' (5), both of which charted in 1978.

5

classics about love turned poisonous, but he was marketed to the new wave rock audience as if he was from the same bloodline. When the Sex Pistols fell apart in early 1978, the new Elvis was summoned to Thames TV's *Today* studio, where the Pistols once turned the air blue. Asked what their split meant to him, Costello answered that it didn't mean much at all, and that he had no idea why he'd been invited onto the programme.

Much of the early new wave was a motley assortment of hangovers and newcomers, people too old/odd/ill fitting to be called 'punks', but still opposed to the old dinosaur bands. Squeeze were a raucous but traditional bar band out of south-east London, named after the last Velvet Underground album (the one without Lou Reed). Initially marketed like a punk band, with an EP produced by ex-Velvets John Cale on Mark P's independent label Deptford Fun City, they soon found an identity as post-Beatles powerpoppers with bittersweet London lyrics.

Some of the R&B/pub-rock bands that predated punk found themselves marketed under the same umbrella. Eddie and the Hot Rods were the classic are-they-or-aren't-they-punks? band for the mainstream audience. The Essex quintet even had their *Teenage Depression* album cover featured as a prop in Derek Jarman's apocalyptic punk film, *Jubilee*, but one look at the longish hair and flared jeans on the cover of their *Live At The Marquee* EP told the punks all they needed to know. The Hot Rods' main significance lies in how the Sex Pistols gained attention as their support band, by trashing the headliners' equipment and pissing them off.

Also seen as 'new wave' by default, the Tom Robinson Band (or 'TRB', to give the band its acronym) was a rather stodgy mainstream rock group. Well-spoken nice guy Robinson distinguished himself via the most overtly left-wing sentiments outside of The Clash, and numbers like the radical cabaret song 'Sing If You're Glad To Be Gay'. The effect was that of a pub rock band led by a hectoring social worker. It's amusing to look back at how young punk Stalinists Julie Burchill and Tony Parsons ended their book *The Boy Looked at Johnny*, a speed freak's 'Obituary of Rock 'N' Roll', with a tribute to the only band that they thought mat-

Numerous garage-rock singles came under the umbrella of 'new wave': Wreckless Eric recorded his classic 'non-hit' 1977 debut 'Whole Wide World' (1) for Stiff – note his Barney Bubbles-designed logo. Further singles followed, like 1978's 'Take The Cash' (2, Spanish edition), but, despite the Oh Boy-style extravaganza of the cover, alcoholism beckoned to the frequently wrecked Eric. The Flys were briefly signed to EMI in 1978 for catchy powerpop tunes like 'Fun City' (3), but soon had their ambitions swatted.

The 'new wave' brought a plethora of former pub rockers on its crest: The Hammersmith Gorillas were an R&B band who recorded a cover of the Kinks' 'You Really Got Me' (4, Spanish version) in 1977, but their label adorned it with safety pins and marketed it as 'punk-rock'. Eddie and the Hot Rods had more in common with Essex R&B godfathers Dr Feelgood; their 1976 Live At The Marquee EP (5) featured garage-punk standards '96 Tears' and 'Gloria', but they went down in history as the band who had their equipment trashed by the Pistols.

Squeeze's 1977 debut Packet Of Three EP (6) was released on Mark P's Deptford Fun City label; the characteristically jokey band line-up on their 1978 chart hit, 'Take Me, I'm Yours' (7, Spanish edition), features future TV host Jools Holland (far right), perfecting his junior Groucho Marx shtick. The Count Bishops recorded 'Baby You're Wrong' (8) for pub rock champions Chiswick in '77, but shortening their name to 'the Bishops' for 1978's 'I Take What I Want' (9) raised their profile not a jot. Roogalator were the funkiest of the pub rock bands, their 1977 cut 'Love And The Single Girl' (10) eclipsed rather than showcased by punk.

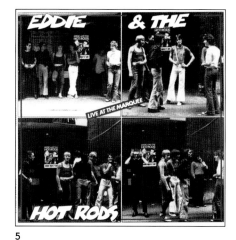
5

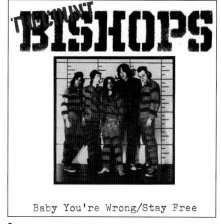

Baby You're Wrong/Stay Free

8

PACKET OF THREE
6

9

4

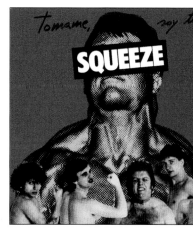
7

10

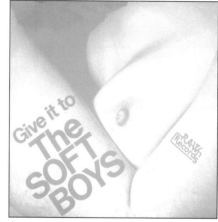

The fist punching the air suggested the radicalism of The Clash, but the Tom Robinson Band's 1977 debut, '2-4-6-8 Motorway' (1) sounded like Status Quo with a middle class vocalist. The TRB's political stance was born out by 1978's Rising Free EP (2), featuring the courageous 'Sing If You're Glad To Be Gay' and their unpunky 'new wave' audience on the cover; 'Up Against The Wall' (3) railed against civil service politicos, but its pic sleeve originated a rumour that Benny from BBC kids' show Grange Hill was the cover star. A 1977 new wave oddity, the Give It To The Soft Boys EP (4) introduced the nouveau psychedelic band of that name; vocalist/guitarist Robyn Hitchcock would make a career out of his unique brand of English whimsy. The Only Ones rode no other wave but their own, seen on the cover of their 1977 debut, 'Lovers Of Today' (5); their classic 1978 hit 'Another Girl, Another Planet' (6) is an ambiguous love song that may be about heroin, the drug that wiped charismatic frontman Peter Perrett from the musical map.

2

3

5

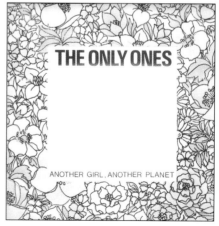

6

Revolutions on Vinyl

tered: the TRB, by virtue of political correctness.

In terms of bands on the fringe, the Stranglers had probably the greatest claim to the epithet 'punk rock'. The murky garage psychedelia of their debut double A-side, '(Get A) Grip (On Yourself)'/'London Lady', sounded like a mutant Brit hybrid of the 1960s *Nuggets*-punk bands. They had a genuinely surly attitude, as evidenced by their band name, leering sexuality and fixation on violence and the macabre. They were the anti-TRB, even recruiting strippers to dance with them on stage. This was seen as passe by many punks and the Stranglers were also chided for their misogyny (some lyrics had an ambiguous attitude to violence against women). But their most fundamental sins were the length of their hair and their age range, from mid-twenties to early forties. The Stranglers were fierce enough to call out the Sex Pistols in their time, and there's little doubt as to who would have come off worse. But the longer they persisted the less value they had, gradually losing their bite and recording a pointless cover of *Nuggets*-era classic '96 Tears' in the 1980s.

At the other end of the age spectrum, The Jam were often roped in with early punk roundups in the music press. The youthful trio from Woking, Surrey had come to London when leader Paul Weller was eighteen. Heavily indebted to the early Who, Swinging Sixties fetishist Weller made outspoken comments about patriotism and how he would vote Conservative in a general election. (The Clash sent The Jam a telegram in response, inviting them to target practice with Maggie Thatcher.) Growing up in public, Weller moved left-of-centre and became one of the best observational British songwriters since Ray Davies of the Kinks.

By the time of their loud and furious 1979 'The Eton Rifles', even Joe Strummer had to admit no one could fashion a single out of British class conflict better than Weller. Along the way, The Jam inadvertently managed to inspire another youth movement, the late 1970s mod revival (slightly precipitated by The Jolt, more 1960s R&B revivalists). Unlike The Jam themselves, the new mods were notable for their collective incapability of producing even one good single.

Also historically linked to the punk movement, The Fall emerged from the ''77 shit pile' in Manchester – at least according to their founder, casually dressed young working man Mark E. Smith. Ever since their debut on Step Forward, 'Bingo-Master's Break-Out!', MES's semi-spoken lyrics have depicted a hyper-real modern Britain, where grotesque characters, conspiracies and ghosts lurk beneath the surface – set to a metallic rockabilly-punk hybrid backing. Regarded by many as the latter-day spirit of punk rock, the cantankerous Smith would probably despise the accolade.

As significant as The Fall in terms of the birth of 'art-punk', Wire were an urgent quartet whose brevity (their classic 'Dot Dash' is over within two minutes) and proletarian-sounding vocals (listen to 'I Am The Fly') may have suggested punk fundamentalism to some. But their lyrical viewpoint, like absurd conceptual snapshots of the modern world, was reflected in the almost Dadaist approach to their pic sleeves. Tellingly perhaps, they were signed to Harvest, EMI's prog-rock label, becoming progressively more esoteric and experimental until they began to split and reform with regularity.

One of the more cerebral figures to come out of UK punk, Buzzcocks defector Howard Devoto returned to the podium in 1978 with Magazine. While their classic debut, 'Shot by Both Sides', lifted an ascending guitar motif from early Buzzcocks song 'Lipstick', Magazine rejected punk's now dogmatic primitivism to incorporate a broader set of references: electronics; soundtrack music; a literary sensibility rooted in Penguin Modern Classics territory. Appositely, some of the pic sleeve illustrations (by Devoto's onetime lover, Linder Sterling) evoked a sense of both fascination and unease.

Devoto caught flak from some of his more politicised contemporaries, for failing to tow the socialist line and describing states of mind that verged on nihilism. Compared to one of his more disreputable (and, latterly, more famous) contemporaries, however, he was virtually PC.

Adam Ant, the future Prince Charming of pantomime pop, first came to attention as a nihilist punk

1

2

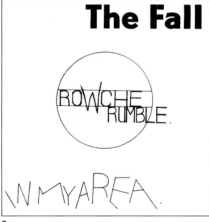

3

A new wave all of their own: catalysed by the Manchester punk explosion, The Fall released 'Bingo-Master's Break-Out!' (1) on Step Forward in 1977, the same year that they formed; its grotesque cover drawing suggests the inner workings of an unhinged mind, an internal landscape that vocalist/ lyricist Mark E. Smith traverses to this day. On 1978 and '79's 'It's The New Thing!' (2) and 'Rowche Rumble' (3), their garage-band ethos and Smith's unpretentious artistry are reflected in the sub-Letraset typography.

1

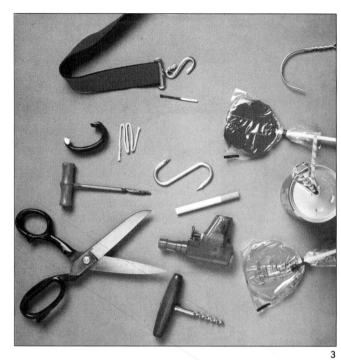

3

2

4

5

6

7

8

Art goes Pop!/Punk goes Art!: West Country band XTC surfed the new wave in 1977 with 'Science Friction' (1, German edition). Their quirky, jerky pop-art ethos is reflected in the covers of 1978's 'Statue Of Liberty' (2) and 'This Is Pop' (3); 'Making Plans For Nigel' (4), with its parody board game illustration by Jill Mumford, was their emblematic post-punk hit in 1979 before leader Andy Partridge retreated to the strawberry fields of Beatlesque psychedelia. Virgin stablemates Magazine were a different kettle of piranha, post-punk existentialists. Both their classic 1977 debut, 'Shot By Both Sides' (5), and 1978's 'Give Me Everything' (7) featured surrealistically evocative cover illustrations by Abstruse Images, like a meeting between the imaginations of Mervyn Peake and H. P. Lovecraft. The utilitarian typographic design of 'Touch And Go' (6) is by Malcolm Garrett, usually associated with vocalist Howard Devoto's previous band, the Buzzcocks, while the prismatic repetition of 'Rhythm Of Cruelty' (8) from 1979 suggests a Rorschach test.

 Revolutions on Vinyl

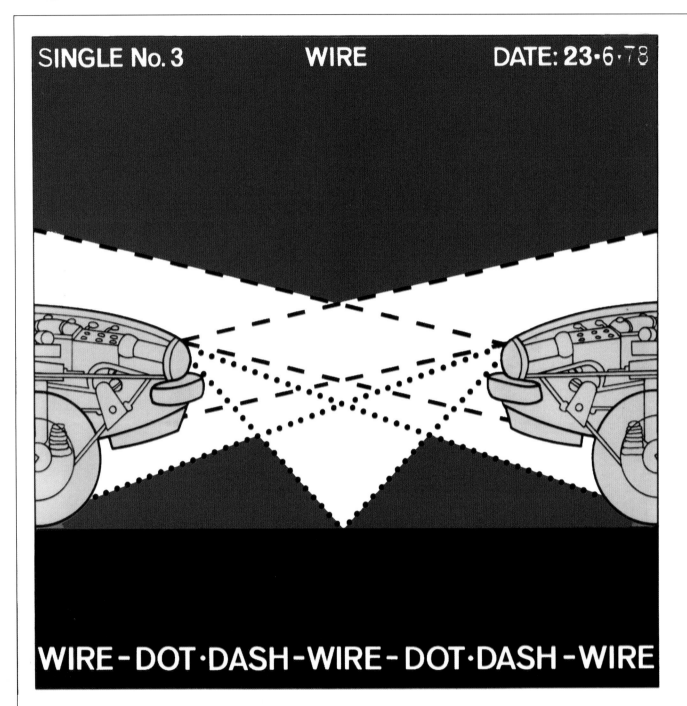

PUNK ON 45

According to artist and designer Russell Mills, Wire were 'the most interesting and uncompromisingly original of the UK punk bands'. Mills later became a regular collaborator, but their early singles exhibit the re-contextualising of found images that is the hallmark of conceptual art. Their 1977 debut 'Mannequin' (2) is self-explanatory, the same picture assimilated into the grid of images for 1978's 'I Am The Fly' (3); released the same year, 'Dot Dash' (1) takes diagrams from a car manual while 1979 single 'Outdoor Miner' (4) prints a photo of a leopard in negative; 'A Question Of Degree' (5) and 'Map Ref. 41°N 93°W' (6) appropriate an antique photo of a catatonic mental patient and an airforce comand map respectively. Whatever new meanings there are exist in the gap between the songs and the pic sleeves. Little wonder that, despite the ragged punk sound of much of their early music, Wire were signed to EMI's prog-rock label, Harvest.

WIRE
MANNEQUIN
FEELING CALLED LOVE
12 X U

2

WIRE OUTDOOR MINER

4

21 WIRE

I AM THE FLY

HARVEST

3

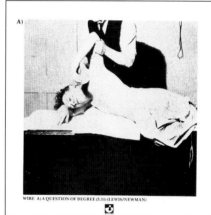

A)

WIRE. A) A QUESTION OF DEGREE (3.11) (LEWIS/NEWMAN)

5

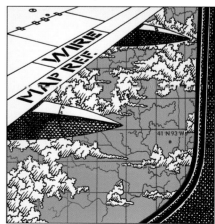

WIRE MAP REF.

41 N 93 W

6

who crossed the borders of moral transgression. Like Joe Strummer with the 101'ers, Stuart Goddard (the future Adam) had a Damascene conversion when confronted with the Sex Pistols. As a member of R&B band Bazooka Joe he was there at the very start, the 1975 debut gig by the Pistols at the Chelsea School of Art. The new young punks on the block were the support band, antagonising both Bazooka Joe and the audience.

Goddard was blown away, but it took a while for him to be reborn as Adam Ant (inspired by 1960s fantasy TV series *Adam Adamant*). With the clanging, metallic original Ants, he sang about sadomasochism and Nazi war criminals, claiming at one point that his personal heroine was Ilse Koch, the 'Bitch of Buchenwald' – 'a vamp in a concentration camp'. They attracted a hardcore following, but, like the Banshees (with whom they played an early double-headliner gig), had their recording career delayed by a right-on squeamishness that affected even the smaller independent record labels. By the time of their 1978 debut single, the incredibly fey 'Young Parisians', disinterested onlookers may have wondered what all the fuss was about. But Adam had constructed a sinister mystique, which he made use of in the film *Jubilee*, and the most calculatedly offensive parts of his repertoire were restricted to his live act. (S&M ditty 'Whip In My Valise' made the second B-side, but the much stronger meat was never committed to vinyl.) Like many members of the punk generation, Adam had begun a continuing process of self-reinvention.

S&M art-punks Adam and the Ants performed for almost two years before cutting their 1979 debut single, 'Young Parisians' (1) . At least the black leather and riding crop give the right hint of transgression – although the Italian edition (2) disappointingly combines the Eiffel Tower with a punk visual cliché, the razorblade. Their first single for the independent Do It, 'Zerox' (3), was a more urgent piece of pop-rock, but, despite the expressionistic cover, the sinister material was still confined to the B-side. Describing himself as a 'Zerox' (sic) machine, Adam was a self-confessed stealer of images who would later transform into a pop-tart dandy highwayman.

2

3

1

CHAPTER 5
PLASTIC PUNK

And this is where things get ugly – if not incredibly silly. 'Punk' moved so quickly from being a groundswell of youthful creativity to a set of ground rules (speed, aggression, brevity, profanity, 'streetwise' attitude) that it invited parody. 'Plastic punks' – like 'plastic gangstas' in the 21st century – adopted the affectations without any of the substance. And who more plastic back in the day than Bertrand?

Plastic Bertrand's 'Ca Plane pour moi' is one of the most recognisable bad records of the era. A European and stateside hit in 1977, it had teenagers who didn't take punk too seriously mouthing its catchy 'oo-ee-oo-oo' refrain and the Franglais-gibberish lyrics. This opportunistic young Belgian (nineteen at the time) was quick off the mark in taking punk to the bubblegum market, but the original song he used as a template is a pretty good garage-rock record. 'Jet Boy, Jet Girl' by Elton Motello alludes to bisexuality and S&M, with the

The Vibrators 1977 cut 'London Girls' (1) depicts the popular look among young women who jumped on the punk bandwagon – much as the band themselves were accused of doing.

chorus running, 'He gives me head!' instead of, 'Ca plane pour moi!' (Bertrand's lyric translates as 'That's Why I'm High', with lines of nonsense about his cat psychedelic yawning.) Motello was an expatriate Brit decamped to Belgium, a former bandmate of Brian James, later of The Damned, in a mid-1970s band called Bastard. In 1978, James' former Damned mate Captain Sensible would cover the original 'Jet Boy, Jet Girl' with King, his short-lived band featuring members of the Saints, Chelsea and Johnny Moped. Motello also bequeathed Bertrand his B-side, 'Pogo Pogo', putting him further down the road of punk pastiche. (Who would have thought the convulsive vertical lunge originated by Sid Vicious would become a dance craze like the Twist?)

If, as Warhol said, 'The best parody is the thing itself,' then Britain was flooded with straight-faced punk parodies in the years 1977-8. Ed Banger and the Nosebleeds shouted and hollered, 'Ain't Bin To No Music School', the eponymous Mr. Banger being the original vocalist of Manchester glam/yob/punk band Slaughter and the Dogs. More surprisingly, the rebel-

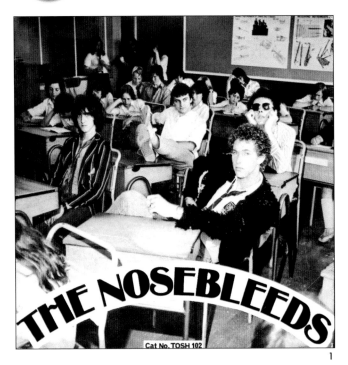

1

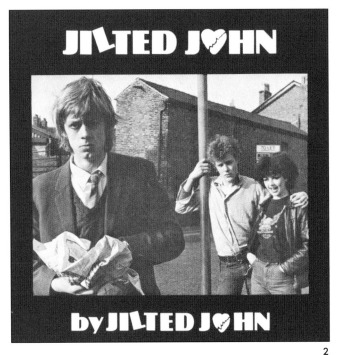

2

3

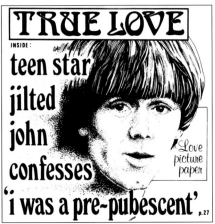

4

5

Released in 1977, 'Ca Plane Pour Moi' (6) was one of the big commercial hits of the punk era – young pop kids scared off by the Pistols' threatening image could sing along with Plastic Bertrand, 'the king of the divan' (and other such nonsense). Bandwagon jumpers the Pork Dukes got in early with 1977's 'Bend And Flush' (3); they were folk rockers who made a part-time career of puerile porn rock. More spot-on was 'Jilted John' (2), the 1978 Buzzcocks parody that found a place in British hearts; post-Julie and Gordon the Moron, the eponymous John didn't score a follow-up hit with 'True Love' (4) in 1979, but creator Graham Fellows went on to a career as a comic actor. Held in similar esteem by their cult following, TV Personalities paid sympathetic tribute to the TV host whose career was ended by the Pistols in 'Where's Bill Grundy Now?', title track of their jangling low-tech 1978 EP (5). Almost an unconscious punk parody, the Nosebleeds' 'Ain't Bin to No Music School' (1), from 1977, bears out its title in shout-along style – only remarkable for featuring Vini Reilly (far left of pic sleeve), who would later lead ambient Factory outfit Durutti Column.

Knox, leader of the Vibrators, was a good ten years older than the original UK punks when his band climbed aboard the bandwagon. But the Vibrators could acquit themselves well with catchy garage pop like 1977's 'Baby Baby' (1), where Knox takes centre place on the pic sleeve. Otherwise, the obvious influence of the 'Orgasm Addict' cover on that of 1978's 'Automatic Lover' (2), and the fact that 'Judy Says (Knock You In The Head)' (3) is all but a Ramones title, show their opportunistic nature.

1

2

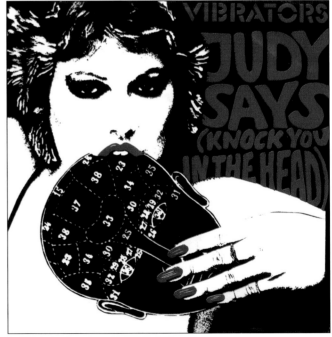

3

lious schoolboys on the pic sleeve featured Vini Reilly, the fragile guitarist who went on to create ambient guitar music with Durutti Column, while one Steven Morrissey (in his pre-Smiths days) would be recruited (and sacked) as second vocalist for a later incarnation of the Nosebleeds. The Pork Dukes were a pastiche mainstream view of what punk was all about, i.e. filth. Their witless, leeringly suggestive records – 'Bend And Flush', 'Telephone Masturbator' – have all the charm of the crudely drawn cartoon showing a young woman fellating a pig. The swinish Dukes were not of the punk generation at all but were three moonlighting folk rockers, two of whom were from Steeleye Span ('All Around My Hat', etc). They were not the only folkies who thought they could pretend to be punks and turn a quick buck: the Monks (featuring ex-members of the Strawbs) had a hit soon after with the execrable 'Nice Legs, Shame About The Face'.

Punk pastiche, when both knowing and affectionate, could still have value. Jilted John, with his auto-biographically-titled single hit, provided a parody of/tribute to the Buzzcocks with his Northern English tale of how he lost Julie to Gordon the Moron. Its rockabilly-backed refrain of 'Here we go – two, three four!' is still remembered fondly. As intimated by the picture sleeves, they also set Graham Fellows (John's creator) on a career as a character actor and comedian, on *Coronation Street* and, latterly, as his own creations, endearingly British losers John Shuttleworth and Brian Appleton.

TV Personalities produced their celebrated *Where's Bill Grundy Now?* EP on their own independent label, Kings Rd. Records. Containing four shambling, jangling tracks that wryly cast an eye over the punk sub culture – including 'Part-Time Punks', speaking to a nation of plastics who affected squalor but had 'still got two-fifty to go see The Clash tonight' – it predated the semi-acoustic 'indie' sound of Orange Juice and the Smiths by several years. The brainchild of Dan Treacy, who styled himself 'Nicholas Parsons' after the quiz show host, they have persisted into the present

4

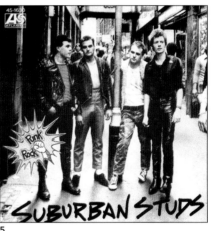
5

Croydon pub band The Banned don't have their hearts in striking the required punk pose for the cover of 1978 single 'Little Girl' (4), their hit cover of the Syndicate of Sound's 1960s garage classic; the Suburban Studs look positively embarrassed to be wrapped around a lamp-post for their 1977 offering 'No Faith' (5).

day via a series of personal traumas, breakups and comebacks.

Punk entered the pop mainstream relatively quickly. Often seen as first-wave opportunists, the Vibrators were a young(ish) group of pub rockers, who coalesced around sometime pop star/session guitarist Chris Spedding on his 'punk' single, 'We Vibrate' for RAK Records, owned by bubblegum/glam impresario Mickey Most. As Spedding climbed off the punk band-wagon, the Vibrators, lead by vocalist Knox, stayed onboard. They were present at seminal events like the 100 Club Punk Festival, while the poppy single 'Baby Baby' testifies that they were an okay garage band. But look at their pic sleeves and see how determinedly they bought into punk: 'Judy Says (Knock You In The Head)', as a title, is redolent of the Ramones' 'Judy Is A Headbanger', while the hybrid of handguns and human figures on 'Automatic Lover' is an approxima-tion of Linder Sterling's graphic style on the Buzzcocks' 'Orgasm Addict'.

Other bandwagon jumpers included the spiky-haired Boomtown Rats, from Dublin, who at least had the good grace to initially deny the punk label. Having more in common with bar bands like Dr Feelgood, leader Bob Geldof later revised his opinion to claim the Rats played the role of pop band on the original punk scene (conveniently discarding the Buzzcocks). As his songs became more grandiose, the records steered in the direction of pomp-pop bands like 10cc or Queen rather than anything punkish. Malnourished Ethiopians who survived the Eighties may have reason to give thanks for the Rats' fading glories.

The Police, too, were originally sold as a punk band, a first foot in the door for their ambitious lead singer. They got their first break as backing band to fellow opportunist Cherry Vanilla, a former New York rock publicist/groupie who traded on her reputation with singles like 'The Punk'. Sting hollered his way through drummer Stewart Copeland's 'Fall Out', the Police's debut release on his brother Miles Copeland's

Illegal Records. Early Eighties pop kids will recognise that Police guitarist Andy Summers is absent from the pic sleeve – the original line-up featuring Henry Padovani instead, prior to their uniform bottle blond look. By the time of their breakthrough single, 'Roxanne', and its shrill 'white reggae' sound, the 'punk' B-side, 'Peanuts', found Sting shrieking about the decline of his former hero, Rod Stewart. It said everything about the Police's punk credentials.

By the end of the 1970s, punk rock was such an established fixture in the UK charts that it spawned punk pop acts like the Members, whose 'Sound Of The Suburbs' combined good-natured shouting and Shadows-style guitar twang. Further down the scale, the fourth division bands adhered to a visual as well as musical template: descended from Roberta Bayley's classic Ramones shots, every other cheap picture sleeve seemed to consist of four guys standing against a wall/in the middle of a high street/against an amuse-ment hall, trying to look tough. Some of the less con-vincingly menacing line-ups seen here include the Banned (a Croydon pub band who covered Syndicate of Sound's 1960s *Nuggets*-punk classic 'Little Girl') and the Leyton Buzzards from north-east London.

Bedecked in Ramones-style biker jackets for their debut EP, the Buzzards wore soul-boy suits on stage. Their stage favourite was an incendiary number called 'Baader-Meinhof Gang' – when their label, Small Wonder, refused to release it for its glorification of vio-lence, they changed the lyric to 'When You're Seventeen'; it later turned up on a John Peel radio ses-sion as 'Disco Romeo'. Their career as a band was sim-ilarly pragmatic: in the early Eighties, most of the Buzzards re-emerged as 'new romantics' Modern Romance with the cocktail-friendly 'Everybody Salsa'; vocalist Geoff Deane hopped aboard a new career as 'style journalist' for 1980s mag *The Face*. Chancers to the last, the Buzzards epitomise those for whom punk was not some nameless gut feeling that needed to be expressed, but simply naked opportunism.

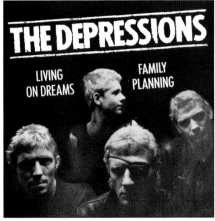

1

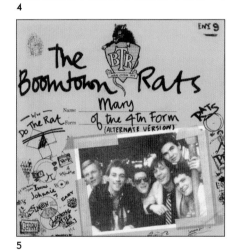

4

2

5

3

6

Career opportunities (the ones that sometimes knock): The Depressions line up like a peroxide Johnny Kidd and the Pirates for 1977's 'Living On Dreams' (1), their dream of garage-punk fame fading with the following year's 'Messing With Your Heart' (2). New town punk band Johnny Curious & the Strangers strike the requisite 'street' pose for their 1978 single 'In Tune' (3), but look like easy prey for twelve-year-old muggers. Venus and the Razorblades were a US female punk band hastily put together by Kim Fowley, godfather of the Runaways. Their debut single was 1977's 'Punk-a-Rama' (4). The Boomtown Rats, while lumped in with 'punk' by the mainstream press, were honest enough to deny the connection at the time of their 1977 single, 'Mary Of The Fourth Form' (5); their biggest hits would come from mainstream pastiches like 1978's 'Rat Trap' (6), a nod in the direction of Springsteen.

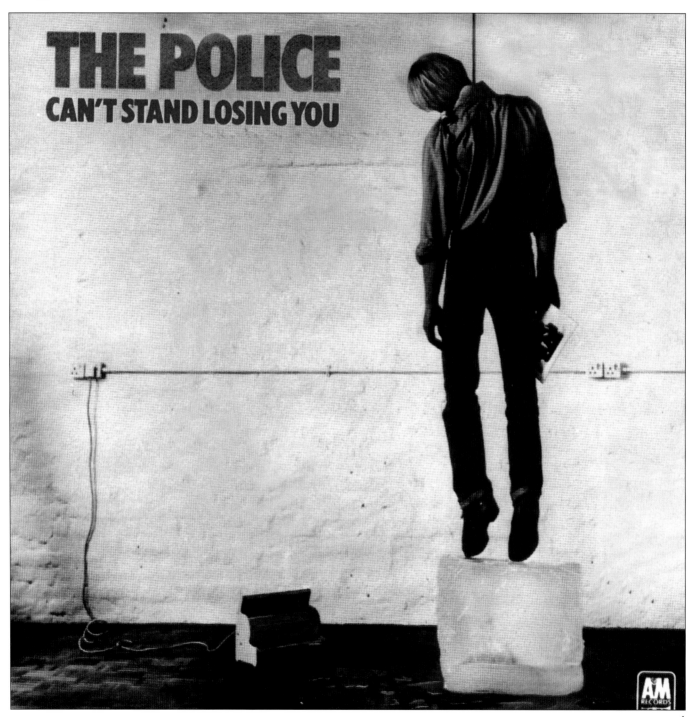

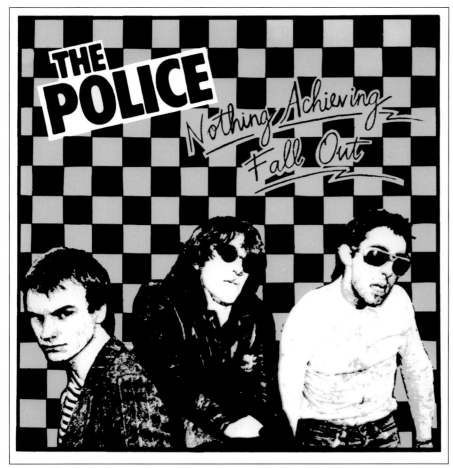

2

3

4

Plastic punks: The Police were briefly a punk band, debuting with their 1977 double A-side 'Nothing Achieving'/'Fall Out' (2); subtract guitarist Henry Padovani (right of pic sleeve), substitute Andy Summers, add several bottles of hair bleach and you have the nascent stars of 1979's 'Can't Stand Losing You' (1), In their new 'white reggae' style. By this time, 'punk' was just another offshoot of UK pop music, as demonstrated by the Members and their 1979 hit 'The Sound Of The Suburbs' (3); the Leyton Buzzards, photographed in Ramonic style outside an amusement arcade for 1978's '19 & Mad' (4), would have a minor hit in poor man's Ian Dury-style in 1979 with 'Saturday Night Beneath The Plastic Palm Trees' (5), before re-emerging as new romantics Modern Romance.

5

1

CHAPTER 6
PUNK AMERICANA

For all the outrage of UK punk, its American counterpart was often a darker, more subversive beast. This was partly due to its underground nature: 1970s punk was never commercially embraced in the way that it was in Britain. (The US assimilation of punk rock would not take place until the early 1990s, when its championing by Nirvana would inject some raggedy-assed rawness back into the mainstream American rock scene.) The transatlantic cultural divide may also have been due to how the youth of (once Great) Britain had an all-too-conscious awareness of fallen empire and their place in its state of decay. For them, it was truly apposite to celebrate the fact that there seemed to be No Future.

In America, the dynamic was different. Nowhere else on earth could the polarity of modern life be experienced at such extremes: the striving for individualism and the tendency towards mindless conformity; the optimistic faith in progress and the reliance on brute

Subverting the norm and de-evolving the species, arch electro-satirists Devo on the cover of their mould-breaking 1976 debut, 'Jocko Homo' (1, UK edition from 1977).

force and weapons; the unshakeable belief in God, the flag and Mom's apple pie, contradicted by some of the most obscene crimes ever committed by citizens of a civilised nation.

Such contradictory realities created a trash culture aesthetic. For the denizens of the USA's regional underground rock scenes, punk rock had a natural role to play in showing how smiley Ronald McDonald was really John Wayne Gacy in full clown makeup. It's an era that belies sneering Brits who refuse to believe that any Americans understand the meaning of the word 'irony'.

Prominent among the cultural deviants were Devo, from Akron, Ohio – one of the most industrialised (and most polluted) cities in mid-America. 'Punk' was an arbitrary label to describe their singular brand of elec tro-pop. First released on their Booji Boy label in 1976, 'Jocko Homo' sounds like nothing that came before and very little that has happened since. Pitched between discordant electro-noise and a marching song, it stated the band ethos of 'de-evolution' (its catch-phrase, 'Are we not men?' taken from classic sci-fi horror movie *The Island of Lost Souls*). It was also accom-

1

2

3

hot wire my heart «» baby you're so repulsive

4

WE ARE . THE ONE

5

Devo's short underground film, The Truth About De-Evolution, was basically an avant-garde promo video. Traces of it can be seen on the pic sleeve of their 1977 cover of the Stones' 'Satisfaction' (1), while 1978's 'Be Stiff' (2) satirically embraces the Readers Digest aesthetic of the 1950s, and 'Come Back Jonee' (3) came with a sticker of a bust of Apollo's head to place over a piece of moonrock. Less conceptual in their satire, the Dickies celebrated blue-collar Americana on their 1978 cover of 'Silent Night' (6). The nascent punk scene they emerged from was more hard-edged, as personified in 1977 by cop-drag nihilists Crime with 'Hot Wire My Heart' (4), which became a punk chart hit when its B-side was flipped in the UK, and the Avengers, whose 'We Are The One' (5) features vocalist Penelope Houston in near-cruciform.

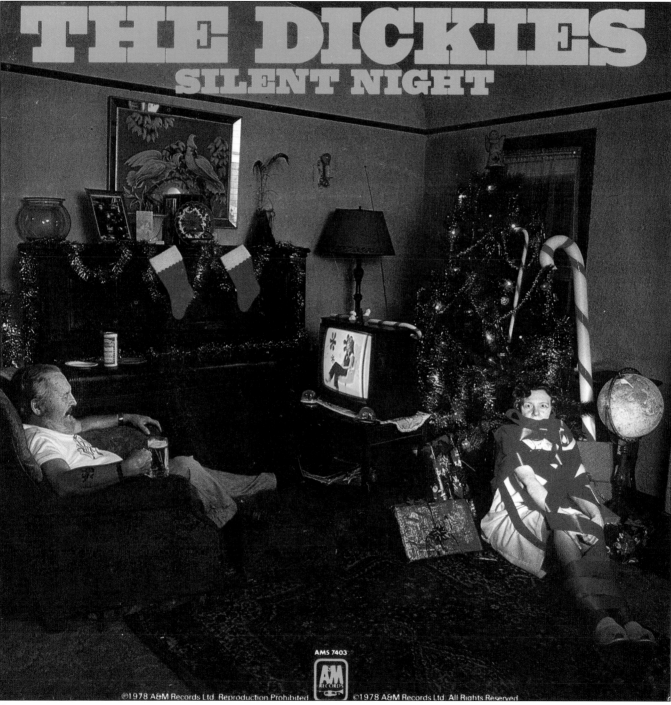

1

2

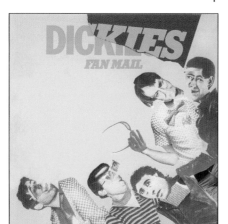

3

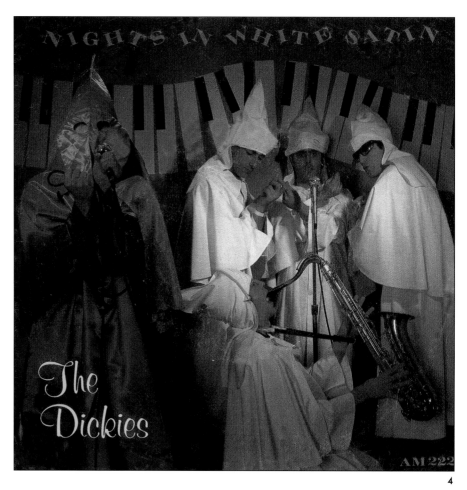

4

The Dickies took absurdist punk to its limit with their 1979 hits 'Banana Splits' (1) and 'Fan Mail' (2); their high-speed cover of the Moody Blues' 'Nights In White Satin' (4) carries a darker overtone, evoking the 'knights' of the KKK. Finger-snapping nihilism was always the bedrock of the Cramps' 'psychobilly' music, married to a strong trash aesthetic: their 1978 cover of the Trashmen's 'Surfin' Bird' (3) and tribute to the daredevil/comic-book character known as the 'Human Fly' (5) carry distinctive typography based on the EC horror comics of the 1950s; on the latter, the band's longterm core of Lux Interior and Poison Ivy Rorschach (centre) almost look like horror-movie stars themselves, distorted by the murky cover image.

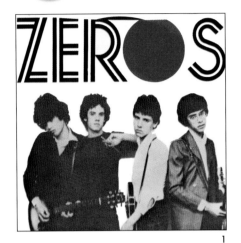

1

2

3

4

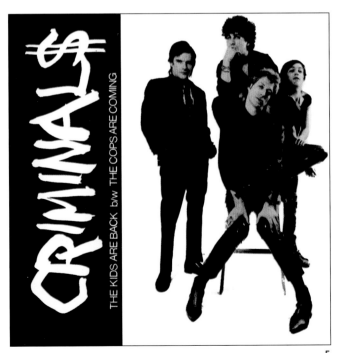

5

The mid-1970s splintering of the New York Dolls sent ex-members in different directions: bassist Arthur 'Killer' Kane teamed up with founding ex-Doll Rick Rivets in the Corpse Grinders, a horror-rock band whose 1978 single 'Rites, 4 Whites' (4) shows their Grand Guignol stage persona, overseen by the vampire from Nosferatu. The Criminals followed a more tuneful garage-rock line with 1979's 'The Kids Are Back' (5), ex-Dolls guitarist Sylvain Sylvain seen perched atop a stool. It was the New York ethos of the time, epitomised in 1977-8 by Hispanic Nuggets-rockers the Zeros' 'Don't Push Me Around' (1), 'Who's Been Sleeping Here' (2) by Tuff Darts, featuring future rockabilly revivalist Robert Gordon, and the Shirts' 'Tell Me Your Plans' (3) — the latter two boasting perhaps the most prosaic cover illustrations of all time.

panied by an innovative amateur video, depicting the band as the sports jocks/geeks on the single sleeve and vocalist Mark Mothersbaugh as (apparently) a wriggling spermatozoa. The flip side of their reverse eugenic philosophy featured on the B-side, 'Mongoloid', a hauntingly catchy story of an everyday guy who has 'one chromosome too many'. It's hard to imagine any touring band recording it now without provoking protests. For a touring band is what Devo became – once de-evolution devolved into a one-note joke, they continued to put out low-tech synth-pop for which the term 'new wave' might have been invented. But their single sleeves remain little pieces of surreal Americana.

More playful but less inventive, the Dickies spewed out a life's worth of US trash culture as a speedy punk thrash, like a comedy version of the Ramones. Avowedly disposable as they were, theirs is a dark perspective on the American Dream, reflected in their 1979 hit album *Dawn Of The Dickies* (after the consumerist satire zombie movie *Dawn of the Dead*) and the sleeve of their cover of the Christmas carol 'Silent Night'. But still, by regurgitating old kids' TV fare like the *Banana Splits* theme tune, the Dickies became the post-Baby Boom generation's favourite pop-punk band.

The macabre was inherent in US punk. Following in the wake of the Vietnam War and the end of the hippie dream that followed the Manson murders, it often embraced darkness rather than (as in the UK) railing against the greyness. If punk attitude meant spitting in the face of both the liberals and the conservative establishment, then it shared much in common with the new wave of US horror movies that began with *The Texas Chainsaw Massacre* (Johnny Rotten's professed favourite comedy)

Relocated to the New York/CBGB's scene from the Midwest via way of Sacramento, CA, the Cramps brought a monochrome taint of Fifties rock'n'roll to the punk scene. According to the liner notes of their early singles collection, 'the group developed its uniquely mutant strain of rock'n'roll aided only by the sickly blue rays of late night TV.' Their debut single, a cover of the Trashmen's sublimely moronic 'Surfin' Bird', was

released in 1978, just a few months after the Ramones' version appeared on their *Rocket To Russia* album. The crepuscular EC horror comic design of their covers continued with 'Human Fly', a rockabilly tribute to a stuntman-cum-comic book character. Throughout the ensuing decade, they would make the hybrid style christened 'psychobilly' their own. The Corpse Grinders ploughed a similar murky furrow, though their music was more conventional (as opposed to retro) rock'n'roll. Taking their name from a 1970 schlock-horror comedy that was surely a Cramps favourite, they featured ex-New York Dolls Arthur Kane and Rick Rivets and played horror rock not a thousand miles removed from Alice Cooper – who had given Rivets' previous band, the Brats, their name.

Horror rock continued apace with the Misfits – a cult band for three decades, their original incarnation featured muscular vocalist Glenn Danzig crooning like a demonically possessed Elvis. Danzig would later lead his eponymous heavy metal band further into occult fantasy, while the Misfits reformed with a new vocalist and lashings of ghoul paint. The Plasmatics, a noisily theatrical metal-punk band, were chiefly notable for the spectacle of chainsawing a car in two on stage and singer Wendy O. Williams' improvised cleavage: two strips of duct tape across her nipples. There's a macabre overtone in the guitarist's Leatherface-type mask on the cover of 'Butcher Baby', but it's as nothing compared to the horror of Ms Williams' shotgun suicide in 1998.

Shock-horror aesthetics aside, American punk remained as bafflingly broad a church as it had been during the early CBGB's scene. On the West Coast, the San Francisco punk scene centred on the Mabuhay Gardens venue, as chronicled in the seminal US 'zine *Search & Destroy* (edited by V. Vale, later founder of the innovative Re-Search publishing house). Prominent on the scene were Crime, whose don't-give-a-shit attitude came in the authoritarian drag of San Francisco Police Department uniforms. Minimalist and crushingly loud, a British pressing of their 1976 cut 'Baby You're So Repulsive' won a place in the UK new wave charts before their appeal wore thin. The Avengers played fast, loud and tinny, much in the style of the Dictators, distinguished by female vocalist Annie Golden. Their moment in punk history came when they supported the Sex Pistols at the fated Winterland gig in early 1978. Despite Pistols guitarist Steve Jones' production of their subsequent album, the Avengers, like Crime (who had the distinction of being around long before the late Seventies punk scene), faded with the moment.

Back in New York City, things were as diverse as ever. The second generation of CBGB's bands were still pigeonholed as 'punk' by default: the Tuff Darts, featuring future rockabilly icon Robert Gordon, were basic garage rock, as were the Zeros, a group of Hispanics who fetishised the original *Nuggets* punk era; the Shirts were melodic powerpop, as were the Criminals, led by ex-New York Doll Sylvain Sylvain.

Most imposing and most impressive were the delicately named Snatch, the collective title for New York duo Patti Palladin and Judy Nylon. As aggressively glamorous as they appear on their pic sleeves, their musical heritage was equal parts girl bands like the Ronettes and noisy trash merchants like the Dolls. Snatch would decamp to London, where their short-term popularity facilitated collaborations with artists as diverse as Brian Eno and ex-Doll Johnny Thunders. But back in New York, a fierce young performer would epitomise the untamed anima of the post-punk woman. The nineteen-year-old Lydia Lunch, seen on the cover of Teenage Jesus and the Jerks' 1979 'Orphans', earned her nickname by providing food for the Dead Boys when she worked as a waitress (also providing vocalist Stiv Bators with other oral favours on stage). Teenage Jesus were among the noisiest and most nihilistic of the oft atonal post-punk bands known as 'No Wave', recorded by Eno for the album *No New York*. It set the predatory and intelligent Ms Lunch on an extraordinary career path that would produce post-punk music, film, literature and spoken word performances.

No Wave was nihilistic, but still had an artistic, almost conceptual ethos to it. By the late 1970s, however, there was a more fundamentally brutal offshoot of punk gestating in the West Coast underground. The Germs were a grinding LA metal-punk band whose provocative nature can be seen on the cover of 'Forming', where the stars and stripes of Old Glory are hung upside down. Leader Darby Crash was the nearest thing to a US equivalent of Sid Vicious, whose nihilistic lifestyle ended with a heroin overdose in 1981, aged 22. (Crash is the subject of a biography titled *Lexicon Devil*, after one of the Germs' songs.)

Meanwhile, to the north of the Pacific Highway, another prototype hardcore band formed with a more socially aware agenda. The Dead Kennedys were fronted by Jello Biafra, whose absurd stage name evokes both junk food and the Nigerian Civil War massacre. Biafra, who dates the origins of the hardcore punk scene to the first time the Ramones played San Francisco, had written a ditty about Jerry Brown, Governor of California, entitled 'California Uber Alles' – as can be gleaned from the pic sleeve, Brown was satirised as a liberal fascist whose smug old hippie philosophy would force kids to meditate in school. Politically outspoken through the original Kennedys' existence and beyond, Biafra would later target the Republican plutocracy that dominates modern US politics. ('California uber alles indeed,' he commented when Teutonic action hero Arnie Schwarzenegger was elected governor.)

The Kennedys' debut was released on Alternate Tentacles, an independent label seminal to the fertilisation of hardcore. Another was SST, which first gave voice to the brutal, grinding, hardcore attack of Black Flag. Their debut single, 'Nervous Breakdown', featured a sleeve cartoon depicting an angry youth, ready to blow, and his humpbacked teacher. Such personal and intergenerational conflict was a recurring theme for Black Flag (named after an insecticide spray), continuing when original vocalist Keith Morris, and his replacement Dez Cadena, passed the baton down to young fan Henry Rollins. They spoke for a generation of alienated young people who sought no solace in melody, but only catharsis through the violence of bludgeoning noise. Fans and bands alike were crude, disaffected and profoundly pissed off. Their music was punk rock reduced to ground zero.

1

2

3

Angry women: sex-and-chainsaws symbol Wendy Orlean Williams is seen on the cover of the Plasmatics' 1978 'Butcher Baby' (1), with guitarist Richie Stotts in a 'gimp' bondage mask. The formidable Judy Nylon, half of female duo Snatch, had her face on one side of the covers for their 1977 debut 'Stanley' (2), while a sultry Patti Palladin graced 1978's 'All I Want' (3). Their direct descendent, a young Lydia Lunch, stares out from the cover of Teenage Jesus and the Jerks' 1979 single 'Orphans' (4), her diminutive stature masking a woman not to be messed with.

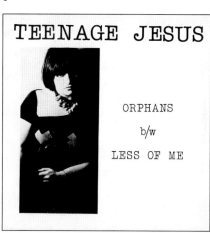

4

*The American Nightmare:
The Dead Kennedys'
1979 debut 'California
Uber Alles' (1) satirised
Governor Jerry Brown as
a liberal fascist presiding
over smiley Nuremberg
rallies for health food
fans. US punk's Dadaist
use of found imagery
found its apogee in
(naturally) the Dadistics'
'Paranoia Perception' (2),
while an image of the US
military-industrial complex,
apparently straight from
the pages of Scientific
American, took on
apocalyptic overtones for
the Weirdos' 1978
offering 'We Got The
Neutron Bomb' (3). The
US hardcore scene took
its first brutal steps with
the Germs' 1977 Forming
EP (4), the self-destructive
Darby Crash standing
before an upside-down
US flag, and Black Flag's
1978 debut 'Nervous
Breakdown' (5) with its
comic-book image of
intergenerational conflict.
1979's 'Night Of The
Living Dead' (6), by the
original Misfits, was a
limited edition of 2,000
given away at a
Halloween show,
featuring a doctored still
from the eponymous
movie, while the Urinals'
self-titled debut EP (7)
had such a
primitive Xerox design
that they must have
been taking the piss.*

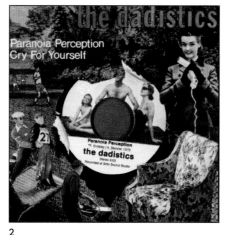

2

5

3

6

4

7

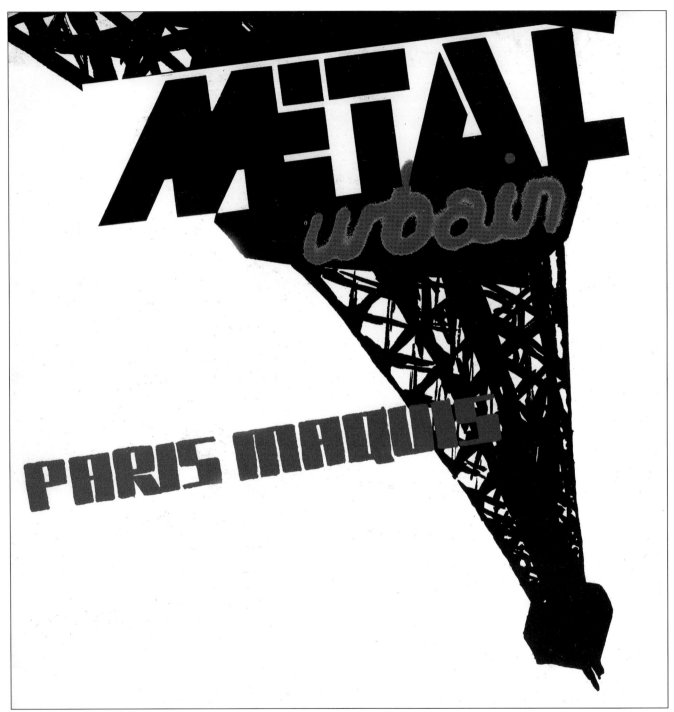

CHAPTER 7
GLOBAL PUNK

If evidence were needed that punk was a series of simultaneous pop-cultural accidents, rather than a cohesive movement, the Saints provided it. Formed in conservative Brisbane, Australia in early 1976, they were blissfully unaware of anything called 'punk rock'. Their first single, '(I'm) Stranded', was recorded as a demo but released by EMI Australia in October '76 – technically preceding The Damned's 'New Rose', the first UK punk single. Like the Pistols and the Ramones, the Saints came up with a raw template that rejected the flaccidity of the mid-Seventies rock scene: the disaffected vocals of Chris Bailey; the snarling buzzsaw guitar of co-writer Ed Kuepper; the lyric that pointed – like so many Pistols songs and the Buzzcocks' 'Boredom' – to a nowhere, a void, that the song's narrator was unable or unwilling to escape.

'Paris Maquis' (1) by Metal Urbain became the first record released by Rough Trade in 1977. With their electro-punk sound and industrial imagery, this underrated band pointed to the post-punk future.

With the British punk explosion, the Saints found themselves a readymade market. Their debut album, also called *(I'm) Stranded*, was an R&B-based collection of unlucky-in-love songs. But it had speed and attitude, and hit the racks before any of the UK punk bands had delivered their first album. When the Antipodean foursome decamped to the mother country, however, disillusion set in. The problem lay in the image on the pic sleeve: there's a slouching surliness in evidence, but paunchy singer Bailey and balding Kuepper look more akin to pub rockers than anything the London demimonde deemed 'punk'. Over such trivialities did a promising band flounder. They released one more classic single, the snarling, nihilistic 'This Perfect Day', which had the distinction of debuting on *Top of the Pops* the same night as the Pistols' 'Pretty Vacant'. Unlike the Pistols, however, the Saints immediately took a tumble down the charts. Their album of the time, *Eternally Yours*, found echoes in the brass-backed, Stax-influenced sound of Dexy's Midnight Runners several years later. But the

Revolutions on Vinyl

PX 242

1

The Saints didn't know they were a punk band when they were recording '(I'm) Stranded' (1) in 1976, but the Australians' buzzsaw ballad was as timely as the Ramones and the Pistols; 1977's 'Erotic Neurotic' (2, Italian edition) was a rip-off of the Beatles'/Stones' 'I Wanna Be Your Man', while the snarling 'This Perfect Day' (3) was not quite the hit that this German edition boasted of, reaching no. 34 in England. 'Le punk' was a difficult creature to define in France: Fresh-faced Parisians Stinky Toys played the September 1976 100 Club Punk Festival, but their 1977 offering 'Boozy Creed' (4) was tired old rock-a-boogie. Much more radical were Metal Urbain, with 'Panik' (5); under the collective pseudonym of Doctor Mix, their pounding 1979 electro version of the Stooges' 'No Fun' (6) became a cult classic. Even those who don't speak the lingo can spot the darkness inherent in Les Olivensteins 1978 Fier De Ne Rien Faire EP (7) – the appropriated image alluding directly to vivisection.

2

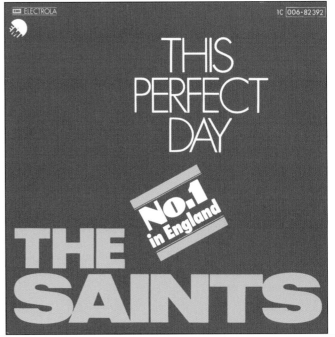

3

4

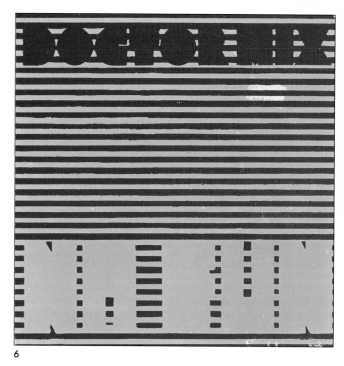

6

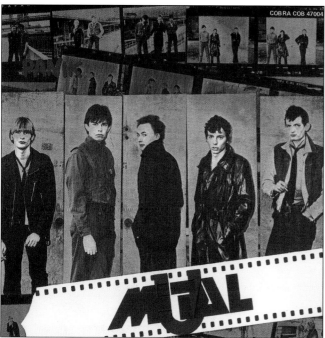

5

7

1

Kleenex were an early Rough Trade band, atypical Swiss girls playing discordant guitar riffs, seen on the gatefold cover of their 1978 debut 'Ain't You' (1); the geometric designs on this and 1979's 'You' (2) were emblematic of the new post-punk modernism. Other Euro-punks were less innovative: Briard, from Finland, were 'Rockin' On The Beach' in 1979 (3), their cartoonishness apposite for a band who had a member decamp to Hanoi Rocks; the Rude Kids may not have been great on grammar, but their 1978 single 'Raggare Is A Bunch Of Motherfuckers' (4) at least threw down the gauntlet to the Swedish biker gang who routinely beat the crap out of punk kids; 'Hot Love' (5) was recorded in 1977 by the first Swiss punk band, but did these moody young men realise the comedy inherent in calling themselves 'the Nasal Boys'?

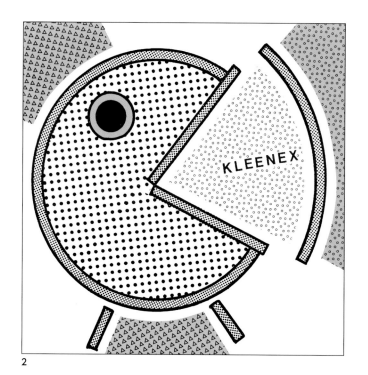

2

4

3

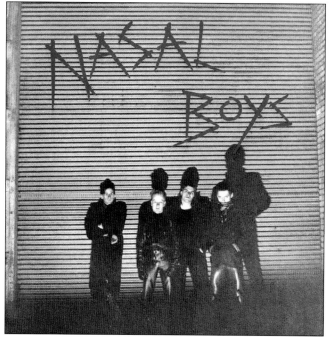

5

original Saints split in 1978, only receiving true recognition of their worth in the decades that followed.

As to what internationally constituted 'punk rock', at first the definition was wide open – the quaintly-named Stinky Toys, a French band, played the 100 Club Punk Festival in London during September 1976, and briefly won a recording deal with Polydor. But, despite the photogenic appeal of vocalist Elli (Medeiros, latterly a girlfriend of film director Brian De Palma), the Toys were a standard R&B boogie band. For a city in thrall to the seedy romanticism of US/British rock'n'roll's most decadent figures, Paris was less convincing when it came to creating its own indigenous brand of 'le punk'. The notable exception to all the new wave Johnny Hallidays was Metal Urbain. Nihilistic and aloof, the band formed in 1976 at the same time that other punk progenitors were reacting against the rancid rock scene. What set them apart was how, like New York's Suicide, they adopted basic electronic instrumentation into the garage-band format. Their set featured a brimstone-stoked cover of the Stooges' 'No Fun', and they became the first band to be released on London's Rough Trade label in 1978, enjoying regular airplay via UK punk champion DJ John Peel.

Born out of the celebrated independent record store in Portobello Market, Rough Trade would put a wide berth on identikit punk, concentrating instead on innovation and experimentalism – to widely varying effect. Swiss girl duo Kleenex, who first recorded for RT in 1978, also set a precedent for the label. Emblematic of what's now seen as 'post-punk', their guitar lines and rhythms were as angular as the early Gang of Four, and anticipated the earnest feminism of more celebrated RT post-punk bands like the Raincoats.

But when the corporate labels went trawling for punk bands, they tended to net stereotypes. The voracious Polydor also snapped up the Rude Kids, a clean-cut bunch of Swedish boys who played noisily and took Johnny Rotten's adage about obnoxiousness being more interesting than music to heart. They first

1

By 1979, the punk seed that had germinated in New York and London was bearing strange fruit throughout Europe, as is evidenced by Serbian punks Pekinska Patka's 'Biti Ruzan Pamean, I Mlad' (1), which was issued on the Jugoton label. Although the quintet were by no means the first punk band to emerge from that region, their fast, energetic songs were indicative of the post-punk sound subsequently epitomised by Joy Division.

2

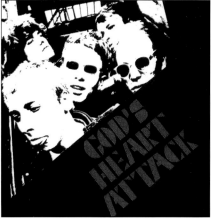

3

4

Nina Hagen was regarded in Germany as the Queen of the Punks – though the eccentric East Berliner had grown out of the European counterculture, assimilating a little psychedelia, a little metal, and even 1979's 'African Reggae' (2). Many Euro-punk bands struck the requisite poses, but made little impression outside their native towns: God's Heart Attack, from Holland, pulled faces in 1978 for 'Treat Me Like A Doll' (3); Hamburg's the Razors slouched Ramonically against a wall for the sleeve of their 1979 single 'Christ Child' (4).

got noticed with the sneering 'We're So Glad Elvis Is Dead', after the world's first rock'n'roll star expired in August 1977. UK release 'Raggare Is A Bunch Of Motherfuckers' was aimed at Sweden's main biker gang but, as its grammar suggests, the main entertainment value of the Rude Kids lay in what was lost in translation.

CBS signed a more original performer, Germany's Nina Hagen, who continues to endure on the Continent. Her main claim to involvement with punk rock seemed to stem from her Siouxsie-ish application of mascara. In reality, she was a young acolyte of the European bohemian/post-hippie scene, who enjoyed a close relationship with Dutch junkie rocker Herman Brood. Her music was eclectic in style, ranging from psychedelic rock to reggae, unified by her eccentric (and rather Euro-centric) lyrics.

Otherwise, the mostly obscure and long-forgotten bands included in this section, ranging geographically from Finland to Canada, were identikit punks: making the noises and striking the poses that were expected of them. Against many shots of backs against walls and surly stances, however, several pic sleeves demonstrate punk's more imaginative use of disturbing visual juxtaposition: 'found' images relating to animal vivisection, tyranny and mass murder.

'Canadian hardcore' may seem an unlikely concept – not so for D.O.A., the first Canadian punk band, whose 1978 Disco Sucks EP (1) is seen here, and who became the first band to have the term 'hardcore' applied to them. Other Canadian punks included the Viletones, whose 1977 single 'Screaming Fist' (2) may or may not suggest their shared leisure activities, and art-rockers the Dishes, who appear, on the 1977 Fashion Plates EP (3), to be the embarrassing nephews that the Monty Python team don't talk about. The DIY punk ethic is in evidence on Lowlife's 1979 single 'Leaders' (4), which equates political leadership with tyranny and murder, cutting and pasting newspaper images of Hitler, Charles Manson, Idi Amin and Rev. Jim Jones.

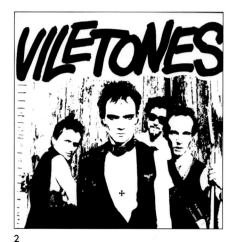

2

3

4

DEATH
DISCO

CHAPTER 8
THE THIRD WAVE
POST-PUNK

If the Sex Pistols were the opening salvo of UK punk, then vocalist John Lydon's (nee Rotten) subsequent band, Public Image Ltd., was the culmination of both its promise and its ultimate failure. Musically, early PiL were far more radical than the Pistols ever were, almost slipping the confines of rock music while staying with the voice/guitar/bass/drums format. Heavily influenced by German experimentalists Can and dub reggae, with Lydon's voice used as a fourth instrument, they were, to coin a cliché, post-punk.

While 'the Sex Pistols' became a corporate umbrella term denoting whatever combination of Cook, Jones and A. N. Other (occasionally Vicious) that McLaren was manipulating for the *Great Rock 'N' Roll Swindle* movie, and Matlock headed toward oblivion in power-pop band the Rich Kids, PiL were looking toward the future. Post-modernism had already infiltrated the artier fringes of punk, but the public image, as it were, of

As with John Lydon's artwork that caricatured the other band members, PiL's 1979 single 'Death Disco' (1) was so far from the Pistols' punk rock'n'roll that it was almost frightening.

PiL was a grassroots variation on the kind of corporate design identity that would permeate the Eighties. Making heavy use of the logo designed by Pistols photographer Dennis Morris, it signified a corporate entity that was, to use another buzz phrase of the ensuing decade, in control. (Or at least that's how they put out. Subsequent recollections by early PiL members Levine, Wobble, Walker or Lee suggest that Lydon was firmly at the helm.)

But the fact that one of punk's luminaries had moved into uncharted waters didn't mean that others were left without a map. By the late 1970s, many had taken punk's promise at its word, street-level kids who formed bands despite their lack of skill or difficult living circumstances. From the same generation as the Pistols, Swell Maps were one of the first dots on the independent map, released on archetypal late Seventies indie label Rough Trade. Their mix of punky brevity, feedback and whimsy made a cult out of their early singles, like 'Read About Seymour', namechecked as a byword for cult coolness in the TV Personalities' 'Part Time Punks'.

3

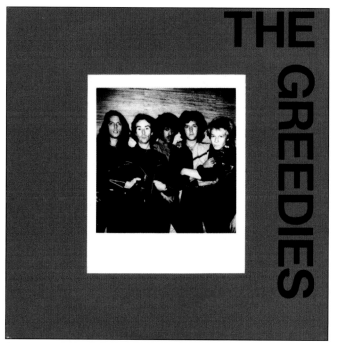

4

More commercially notable among UK punk's third wave were the Undertones, from Derry. Young and brash, they sent John Peel their classic first EP, *Teenage Kicks* on their local independent label Good Vibrations. His incessant playing of the title track landed them a deal with the UK arm of Sire Records (the US label of the Ramones and Talking Heads) and a re-release. Steering clear of any comment on the political situation in their native Northern Ireland, the Undertones were the archetypal working-class kids who saw rock'n'roll as their only open door. Their concerns were teenage crushes or childhood memories, their poppy buzzsaw tunes like a less sophisticated Buzzcocks. Many of their songs haven't aged well, and in the 1980s most of the band split to form My Petrol Emotion, while vocalist Feargal Sharkey embarked on a solo career, followed by a stint as an A&R man. But 'Teenage Kicks' is sublime. Its simplistic riff stutters into life, propelling the two-minute momentum of its tale of adolescent lust, as physically moving as anything in rock'n'roll. Fittingly, it was played at the 2004 funeral of John Peel, the man without whom hardly anyone would have heard of the Undertones (or many far more obscure punk bands).

At the other end of the minimalist scale, bands like the Angelic Upstarts – from the no-bullshit North East – stayed true to what they saw as the political ethos of punk. Accredited as progenitors of the boots-and-bare-knuckles 'oi!' movement, their menacing bonehead vocalist Mensi was no right-wing bootboy but a member of the Trotskyite Socialist Workers Party. Take a look at the *Never Mind The Bollocks*/blackmail letter-style immediacy of their single covers, and feel the permeating tension and violence. In the 1970s, British police forces had a virtual *carte blanche* to treat 'suspects' in whatever manner they chose, as the mainstream press and Middle England refused to countenance the idea of police brutality. The Upstarts made one such instance, 'The Murder Of Liddle Towers', into a local *cause celebre*. (Local boxer Towers had died from internal bleeding following a night in the cells. His case was also championed by Sex Pistols engineer

1

2

3

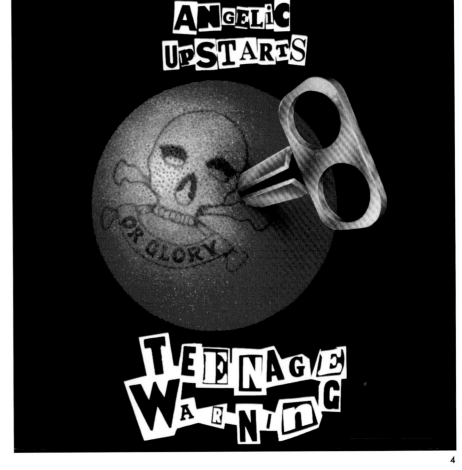

4

Issued in 1978, 'The Murder Of Liddle Towers' (1) is about the case that became a punk rock cause celebre – see 'Justifiable Homicide', previous page. It also marked the debut of the Angelic Upstarts, the aggressive Northern punk band fronted by Mensi, a genuine working-class Trotskyite. The imagery of 1979 singles 'I'm An Upstart', 'Teenage Warning' and 'Never 'Ad Nothin'' (2-4) gives a tense view of late 1970s Britain: frustrated youth; brutal police; urban apocalypse. This was UK punk taken down to its bare bones, predating the even more brutal 'oi!' music.

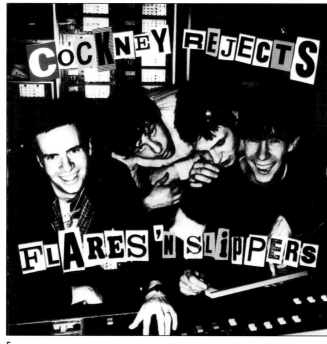

5

Oi oi!: 1979 singles 'Flares 'N Slippers' (5) and 'I'm Not A Fool' (6) were the first two singles by the Cockney Rejects, who made punk conform to their working class conception of street credibility. The sleeve of the former features vocalist Stinky Turner (seen in his 'jamas on 'I'm Not A Fool') and guitarist Mickey Geggus flanking producer Jimmy Pursey (right), of Sham 69, and Garry Bushell of Sounds, who coined the term 'oi! punk'. The Ruts were similarly urgent and aggressive, but had a global political sensibility that set them apart from the nascent oi! bands – as evinced by the primitive op-art of 'Babylon's Burning' (7), the auto-destructive image of 'Something That I Said' (8) and the white Rasta apocalypse prophecy of the reggae-tinged 'Jah War' (9), all of which came out in 1979.

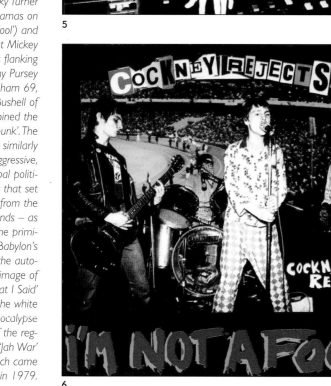

6

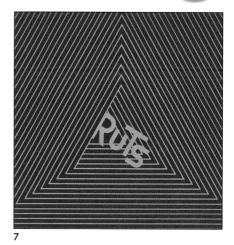

7

8

9

145

1

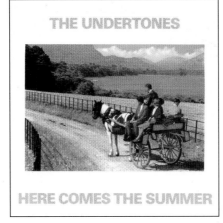

2

3

4

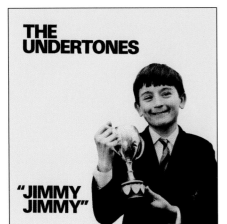

5

6

The Undertones, from Derry, Northern Ireland, were the archetypal street kids for whom rock'n'roll was the way out – seen on the cover of their 1978 classic 'Teenage Kicks' (1, Dutch edition). Pop-punk with colourful pop-art covers to match, 'Get Over You' (2), 1979 singles 'Jimmy Jimmy' (3, with the smiling face of vocalist Feargal Sharkey as a school-boy), 'Here Comes The Summer' (4) and 'You've Got My Number' (5) all celebrate the simple things in life. Their pop-punk sensibility was matched by contemporaries the Revillos – who had changed their name from 'the Rezillos' in 1979 to escape a bad contract, and released 'Where's The Boy For Me?' (6) in a gaudily abstract cover by Ian McIntosh and Sputu.

Young third wavers the Skids debuted in 1978 with the Charles EP (7) before signing with Virgin for the first of a string of singles, 'Sweet Suburbia' (8), with its bizarre comic-book sleeve suggestions of bestiality. Frontman Richard Jobson, seen with big hair and riding boots on the sleeve of the anthemic 'Into The Valley' (9), was a mock-heroic figure fond of showing off his love of European literature. He attracted accusations of neo-fascism in those early PC days, but the Skids' covers utilised found images in a more thoughtful manner than most punk bands: 1979's 'Masquerade' (10) takes the Battle of Culloden and inverts history so that the English lose; 'Charade' (11) features an existential Russian Roulette scenario that might have come from Graham Greene; 'Working For The Yankee Dollar' (12) subverts the flag-raising at Iwo Jima to fit the lyric about US imperialism.

7

10

8

11

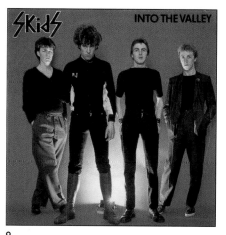

9

12

1

4

7

2

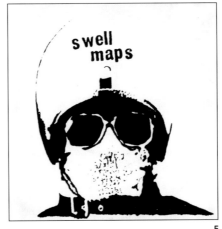

5

3

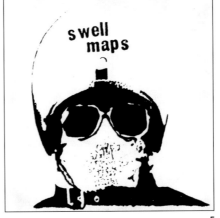

6

'Punk' was difficult to define, but it was often worn as a badge of eccentricity: The Notsensibles were able to claim 'I'm In Love With Margaret Thatcher' (1) in 1979 – when having a right-wing female Prime Minister was still a novelty. Spizz, of Spizz Oil had an apocalyptic comic-book vision evinced on 1978 Rough Trade releases '6,000 Crazy' (2) and the Cold City: 4 EP (3); the first of more than a dozen name changes, to Spizz Energi in 1979, left his vision intact with 'Soldier Soldier' (4), although the sing-along 'Where's Captain Kirk?' (8) was a quirky chart hit. Swell Maps were a garage-band curiosity of early punk, whose 1977 debut 'Read About Seymour' (5) was also a cult single for Rough Trade; despite its found image of a riot policeman, the record had no discernible political content, as was the case with 1978's 'Dresden Style' (6). The eponymously-titled 'The Monochrome Set' (7) married whimsically effete English vocals to its angular style – recorded in 1979, oddly enough, by ex-members of the original Adam and the Ants.

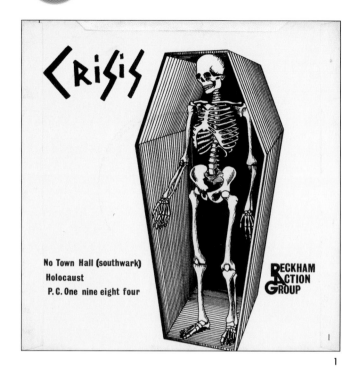

1

3

2

4

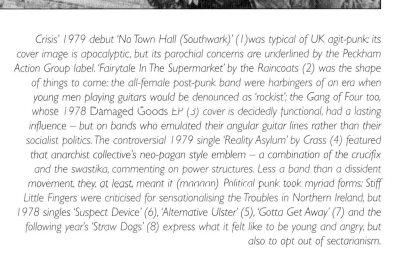

5

6

7

8

Crisis' 1979 debut 'No Town Hall (Southwark)' (1)was typical of UK agit-punk: its cover image is apocalyptic, but its parochial concerns are underlined by the Peckham Action Group label. 'Fairytale In The Supermarket' by the Raincoats (2) was the shape of things to come: the all-female post-punk band were harbingers of an era when young men playing guitars would be denounced as 'rockist'; the Gang of Four too, whose 1978 Damaged Goods EP (3) cover is decidedly functional, had a lasting influence – but on bands who emulated their angular guitar lines rather than their socialist politics. The controversial 1979 single 'Reality Asylum' by Crass (4) featured that anarchist collective's neo-pagan style emblem – a combination of the crucifix and the swastika, commenting on power structures. Less a band than a dissident movement, they, at least, meant it (maaaan). Political punk took myriad forms: Stiff Little Fingers were criticised for sensationalising the Troubles in Northern Ireland, but 1978 singles 'Suspect Device' (6), 'Alternative Ulster' (5), 'Gotta Get Away' (7) and the following year's 'Straw Dogs' (8) express what it felt like to be young and angry, but also to opt out of sectarianism.

2

3

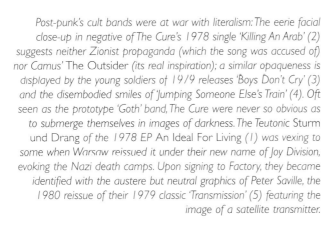

4

Post-punk's cult bands were at war with literalism: The eerie facial close-up in negative of The Cure's 1978 single 'Killing An Arab' (2) suggests neither Zionist propaganda (which the song was accused of) nor Camus' The Outsider (its real inspiration); a similar opaqueness is displayed by the young soldiers of 1979 releases 'Boys Don't Cry' (3) and the disembodied smiles of 'Jumping Someone Else's Train' (4). Oft seen as the prototype 'Goth' band, The Cure were never so obvious as to submerge themselves in images of darkness. The Teutonic Sturm und Drang of the 1978 EP An Ideal For Living (1) was vexing to some when Warsaw reissued it under their new name of Joy Division, evoking the Nazi death camps. Upon signing to Factory, they became identified with the austere but neutral graphics of Peter Saville, the 1980 reissue of their 1979 classic 'Transmission' (5) featuring the image of a satellite transmitter.

5

Revolutions on Vinyl

Dave Goodman and Friends' 'Justifiable Homicide', featuring the distinctive Cook and Jones drums/guitar and ending on a chant of 'Who killed Liddle?')

Possibly the first 'oi!' band proper, the Cockney Rejects, from Canning Town in London's East End, reduced punk to its most 'authentic' elements. Genuinely working class and tough, ex-boxer vocalist Stinky Turner thrived on pure aggression. For the Rejects, 'real punk' was a shout-along accompaniment to fighting with rival football supporters, fighting with the police, fighting in the pub – in short, an accompaniment to fighting. It was punk rock stripped of all creativity, wit and imagination. The Rejects' most recognisable numbers – 'Flares 'N Slippers', 'The Greatest Cockney Rip-Off' – were chanted in playgrounds all over east London, which is perhaps where they belonged. In more recent years, Turner's autobiography received an introductory recommendation from his unlikely champion, Morrissey – nostalgic for an age when young British men regularly fought with their fists and feet, but disdained weapons.

If the Cockney Rejects represented the apolitical and disaffected, then the Ruts imbued the fundamental aggression of punk with apocalyptic urgency. Tense numbers like 'Babylon's Burning' borrowed the imagery (if not the rhythms) of reggae. Popular with many of the same audience who loved the Upstarts and the Rejects, the Ruts were a punk band of the Left, for whom anti-racism and smoking weed were as much articles of faith as amphetamined paranoia had been to the first wave of punk bands. Unfortunately, the desperate state of mind expressed in their first single, 'In A Rut', seemed to mirror vocalist Malcolm Owen's increasing dependence on heroin. After a period off of the drug, his lowered tolerance would kill him when he dabbled again at the start of the 1980s.

Punk was by now an established genre. Ever difficult to define, a certain low-tech irreverence seemed the only real qualifier. Otherwise, it could be fast/slow, left wing/right wing, sombre/silly. In fact there was a school of bands christened 'pathetique punk' by *Sounds'* Garry Bushell, the godfather of 'oi!'. One such

was the Notsensibles, whose absurd shoutalong 'I'm In Love With Margaret Thatcher' appeared on the Snotty Snail label. Played on the Peel show and championed by Bushell, its one-note joke was a crush on the leader of the Conservative Party, elected Prime Minister that same year (May '79). While Mrs Thatcher was a bogeywoman to the Left, there was not yet a recognised ideology called 'Thatcherism' – in the 1980s, however, like 'Reaganism', it would become the bane of any politically inclined punk bands that remained extant.

One of the cult figures on the late 1970s punk scene, the Midlands native known as Spizz inhabited an electronically tinged punk world with distinctly idiosyncratic concerns. Initially under the band name of Spizz Oil, Spizz single covers reflected his fixation with war and militarism, while the lyrics spoke of an eco-apocalypse (the world's resources running down) that, prescient as it seems, wouldn't have been out of place in *2000 AD* comic. With a name change (the first of many) to Spizz Energi, Spizz eventually charted with 'Where's Captain Kirk?' – a shoutalong anthem not nearly as eccentric as the records released by William 'Captain Kirk' Shatner himself.

Inextricably linked with a more earthbound politics, expatriate Northern Ireland band Stiff Little Fingers came to London from Belfast in 1978. Accused by the Undertones of exploiting their country's violent sectarian struggles, SLF (to give them their acronym) retorted that the Derry punk-popsters acted as if 'the Troubles' didn't even exist. Despite the genuine anger and frustration that can be felt in early SLF records, there was an element of truth to the Undertones' argument. Initially a third-wave punk band who took their name from a Vibrators song, leader Jake Burns didn't start writing about the siege state mentality and terror of Ulster until their new manager, Gordon Ogilvie, a journalist from Britain's right-wing *Daily Express*, suggested he should do so. Such opportunism aside, there is a raw abrasion to early singles like 'Suspect Device' and 'Alternative Ulster', and a genuine sense of being sick to the teeth with life in a militarised sectarian society (Burns was a Protestant, but SLF also included

1

Post-punk paranoia: glamsters the Psychedelic Furs covered the Rolling Stones' sardonic 'We Love You' in 1979 (1). Punishment of Luxury debuted in 1978 with 'Puppet Life' (3), its sleeve depicting a cannabalistic nuclear family. The cover of Killing Joke's 1978 debut 'Nervous System' (2) introduced 'the Killing Joke' himself – a Mr Punch dredged up from the depths of the psyche. The Pack would not last into the 1980s, but their confrontational performances and the visceral nature of singles like 1979's 'King Of Kings' (4), with its comment on Christianity, prepared vocalist Kirk Brandon for re-emergence with Theatre of Hate.

3

2

4

Catholics) mirrored in the stark, photojournalistic picture sleeves. They are redolent of a time when it seemed as if the Troubles were truly intractable, and that the bombs and bullets would go on forever.

In mainland Britain, the more politicised punk acts were becoming self-contained communities (most often in the form of communal squats). Seen from our vantage point, their political statements sometimes appear so parochial as to belie the apocalyptic imagery of the covers. London band Crisis's EP may represent death, but its lead track is 'No Town Hall (Southwark)', an attack on municipal politics in the borough directly to the south of the Thames; the track title 'Holocaust' may have suggested more universal concerns, but Crisis still kept it in the 'hood by including the logo of the Peckham Action Group.

Rural Essex anarchist collective Crass managed to build their whole lifestyle around their syndicalist ethos. Initially known for being 'Banned From The Roxy', the song about their barring from the Covent Garden punk club equated the owners not only with fat capitalists, but with the military in Ulster, the murderous Marines at My Lai and the bombers of Hiroshima. With Crass, all roads led to confrontation. When workers at a record plant refused to press their debut EP on Small Wonder, *The Feeding Of The 5,000*, due to the allegedly blasphemous content of the track 'Reality Asylum', the collective responded by forming their own label and issuing it as a single. Set apart from their usual strident shouting, 'Reality Asylum' is a disturbing soundscape that reflects their art student-Dadaist roots, with Eve Libertine's recital blaming 'Jesu' for her sexual repression. Crass were arguably the most significant of the political punk bands, The Clash notwithstanding – for them, it was neither a pose nor a gimmick, but an ideological commitment they maintained

And so the punk era closes with the beginning of the nascent Goth scene. Bauhaus echoed the aesthetic utilitarianism of the architectural movement that gave them their name, but only in their typography. Otherwise their 1979 debut 12-inch, 'Bela Lugosi's Dead' (1) piled on the melodramatics that would define Goth – even though the cover image is taken from a silent film made before the eponymous Lugosi ever essayed the role of a vampire.

until the end. In the early 1980s, the Crass collective, associated bands and artists would form a confrontational anarchist community. It ended with their pre-planned dissolution in the emblematic year of 1984 – and admission from the former anarchist-pacifists that only violence could counter the capitalist/militarist/patriarchal/sexist society they had set themselves in opposition to.

The Raincoats, the feminist post-punk band (complete with caterwauling violinist), released their first single, 'Fairytale In The Supermarket', in 1979. Also at war with patriarchal society, their attack took on a much more self-consciously arty form. One of the archetypal Rough Trade bands, they co-headlined a tour with labelmates Kleenex, the Swiss female post-punk duo. Their screechiness was an acquired taste, and there is a sense that the Raincoats were always preaching to the converted. Still, in the 1990s, Kurt Cobain made it clear to founder member Ana Da Silva that they had been an influence, and precipitated the Raincoats' reformation before his untimely death. The Gang of Four met with a similar fate. Never selling records in any great quantities, by the time of their 1980s split the Sheffield art-punk quartet were already being mooted as an influence by a younger generation of bands – who emulated their taut, angular guitar lines and white funk rhythms, if not their right-on late 1970s politics. In recent years the Gang of Four have reformed, cited as a major influence by the new wave of 'post-punk' bands – particularly Franz Ferdinand.

Though the prevalent ethos of the late 1970s punk generation was socialistic, post-punk embraced all manner of attitudes. Too late (and maybe a little too poppy) to be culled punks, but too raucous for art-punk, the Skids, from Dunfermline, were physically demonstrative young Scots – still in their late teens when they debuted with 'Charles', on the independent No Bad label. Lead singer Richard Jobson had a touch of the young thug about him, tempered by a sartorial style that briefly predated the new romantics, and his boning up on paperback editions of Nietzsche. Signed to Virgin when they came to London, the combination of Jobson's mock-classical lyrics and Stuart Adamson's driving guitar, plus a cover design for their second album that evoked the Munich Olympiad, led to accusations of neo-Nazism. In truth, Jobson wasn't guilty of anything more than youthful egotism (and 'Charles' was a sympathetic lyric about a gay factory worker beaten nearly to death) – but this was the dawn of political correctness, and anyone who didn't toe the left-wing line was automatically suspect.

If the Skids were something of a joke to the arbiters of cultural taste, then Joy Division – a thriving minor cult in their lifetime, a major cult posthumously – were more worrying. The oddly Teutonic name was cribbed by vocalist Ian Curtis from *House of Dolls*, a 1970s paperback (of supposedly dubious veracity) about women forced to prostitute themselves in the Nazi death camps. Their debut EP, *An Ideal For Living* (originally recorded under the name of Warsaw, with its evocation of the ghetto massacres), featured a sketch of what was clearly a member of the Hitler Jugende banging the party drum. Though they never verbally defended their position, Curtis and pals clearly saw a parallel between the *Sturm und Drang* of fascist imagery and the inherent drama of their own post-punk music. By the time of 'Transmission', on Manchester's newly formed Factory label, a manically danceable evocation of nervous breakdown, their heart of darkness had translated into the more austere aesthetic of Peter Saville's cover designs. But there was never any ideology behind the images, merely a willingness to stare into the void and have the abyss stare right back into you. By the time Joy Division made their next classic single, it was a new decade and the song would serve as Curtis' epitaph.

For many of the post-punk bands, the question of politics was somehow beside the point. They had their own visions and their own obsessions to chase, however obscure. The front cover of Killing Joke's 1978 debut single, 'Nervous System', also saw the debut of the 'killing joke' himself – a grotesque Mr. Punch figure, mocking the images of mundanity that his visage was juxtaposed with. This sense of a more sinister real-

ity beneath the surface was symptomatic both of the occult and of psychedelic drugs, aspects that became increasingly associated with Killing Joke throughout the 1980s. Such nightmare visions were common currency then: the illustrated cover of 'Puppet Life', the debut single by post-punk surrealists Punishment of Luxury, depicts a scowling nuclear family devouring a baby for dinner, while a malevolent doll with the face of Punilux's vocalist looks on. Its bland graphic design style, taken from ad brochures and magazines, was subverted to inspire a sense of horror at the mundane.

As the new decade beckoned, the visual aesthetics of the artier post-punk bands continued to make use of found images, but moved further into the abstract and away from any specific meaning. The blank-eyed corpse face of The Cure's debut, 'Killing An Arab', had little to do with the lyric, inspired by Camus' existentialist novel *L'Etranger* (and not, as one pro-Palestinian pressure group insisted, by Zionist propaganda). At the other extreme, the 'positive punk' scene (as it was called at the time 'positive' interestingly equating with the occult and morbid fantasy) could throw up such pieces of literal-mindedness as 'Bela Lugosi's Dead' by Bauhaus, bedecked with monochrome images stolen from a book about horror movies.

In the 1980s, this would lead to the subculture known as 'Goth' which, while ostensibly working from a more imaginative palette, was more rigidly defined than the scattershot iconoclasm of punk. While arguments are made for it as punk rock's successor, it was just one offshoot. In the decade that followed, while mainstream rock and pop music became (in the short-term at least) blander and less threatening, the clashing juxtapositions of punk graphics found more direct echoes in magazine design, or the information overload of 'youth TV', or even in the UK advertising industry, many of whose new wave of designers had been children of the punk generation.

Like the punk era itself, the new graphic styles would evoke a whole range of responses – from shock to cynicism to bafflement. What no one could ever say with any sincerity is that it was 'like punk never happened'.

For almost 30 years now, I have collected Sex Pistols ephemera with a passion. But I have always found the other picture sleeves of the punk era equally compelling and addictive. I have long wanted to compile a book reflecting the magnificent imagery of those few short years – consequently, this book concentrates on the period 1976-79, with a few essential earlier exceptions.

Over the past two years, the production of this book would simply not have been possible without the assistance of the following people: my editor, Dick Porter, who I consulted endlessly; Paul Woods, who wrote the text and captions; Joan Tarpey, who scanned most of the images; Rebecca Longworth, who designed the book; and my publisher, Sandra Wake, who proved as valuable and reliable as ever.

And whilst many dealers worldwide have supplied me with 45s from the punk era, I particularly wish to thank the following: John Esplen, Bill Forsyth, Andy Halstead, Warren Jenkins, Ed Lock, Peter Parzinger, Iain Scatterty, Steve Whitehouse, and John and Kate Willicombe.

And last, but most important of all: 'the Sunday Night Club' (Geoffrey, Hughie, Mossie and Sheamie), Michael Candon and Paul Loftus, both of whom possessed the most musically appreciative ears in Sligo, back in those heady days. They introduced me to a lot of the bands contained herein, at a time when I thought the only light at the end of the tunnel shone from the Pistols' brilliant beacon.

Gavin Walsh (www.whaah.com)

When Gavin Walsh arrived at our offices, with an idea for publishing an anthology of punk/new wave picture sleeves from his collection, one look at the rich and colourful material convinced us. To create a book like *Punk on 45*, however, a team effort is required.

We would like to thank Dick Porter, who, as editor of this book, provided the title, concept and plan, and pooled his amazing knowledge of the period into a close collaboration with the author of the text, Paul Woods.

Thanks are also due to those people who loaned material to supplement Gavin's collection, including Dick Porter, David Walther from www.IanCurtis.org Paul Marco from www.Punk77.co.uk and Paul Woods.

We would also like to pay tribute to the artists who created the records, and the record labels that released them.

Above all, special acknowledgements are due to the designers and graphic artists who created the actual sleeves. Among them are such luminaries as Jamie Reid, Malcolm Garrett, Linder Sterling, Abstruse Images, Jill Mumford, Russell Mills, Barney Bubbles, Phil Smee/Waldo's Design, Dennis Morris/Zebulon, Savage Pencil, Ray Lowry, John Holmstrom, Peter Saville, Ian McIntosh/Sputu, John Luoma Design, Anxious Images, Art On My Sleeve, Ace Productions, Yukio Ishikawa/Harry Lime, Jo Mirowski, Steve Shotter, Cooke Key, Fowler/Coates Ltd, Jules Bates/Artrouble, Simon Ryan, Gal/Daugu/Peronne, Peter Fischli, C. Graves, Bob Last, Peter Dixon, Leee Black Childers, Peter Kodick, Phil Davis, Kevin Sparrow, David Jeffery, D. Broom, Bill Smith, Butch Star, and Megan Green.

It has not always been possible to credit the designer of a particular sleeve, as it was often not documented at the time. Just as integral to this book are the band members who contributed visual ideas, or the anonymous backroom artists who wholeheartedly embraced punk's DIY ethic and Xerox machine culture.

The Publishers